FL

CITIES

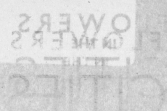

FLOWERS
IN THE
CITIES

The Extraordinary
'DIANA' PROPHECY

Christopher Hill

Marshall Pickering
An Imprint of HarperCollins*Publishers*

Marshall Pickering is an Imprint of
HarperCollins*Religious*
Part of HarperCollins*Publishers*
77–85 Fulham Palace Road, London W6 8JB

First published in Great Britain in 1998 by Marshall Pickering
1 3 5 7 9 10 8 6 4 2

Scripture quotations in the book are taken from the Holy Bible,
New International Version. Copyright © 1973, 1978, 1984 by
International Bible Society. First published in Great Britain 1979,
inclusive language version 1995, 1996. Used by permission of
Hodder & Stoughton, a member of the Hodder Headline Group.
All rights reserved.

A catalogue record for this book is available
from the British Library

ISBN 0 551 03166 2

Printed and bound in Great Britain by
Caledonian International Book Manufacturing Ltd, Glasgow

Contents

Preface

This book was written in response to an invitation by my publishers, HarperCollins*Religious*:

'We'd like you to write a book about the Diana Prophecy!'

My initial reaction was to refuse. It just didn't feel like me. I thought about it. I prayed about it. Then I felt I should do it.

To say it has proved to be a tough assignment would be to understate. It's been *very* tough going! Midnight candles have been burned on many a night.

Through these four months one thing has compelled me to go on – a fast-growing sense that we are living through awesome days. As I tap this into my word processor, news of Iraqi threats of anthrax attacks on London are being contemplated by radio pundits. Am I really hearing this?

The world has gone mad. God help us – nobody else is able to! I pray He will encourage you as you read my little book.

My special thanks are due to my friend Tony Derrick for proof checking so meticulously and to my wife and partner, Lindy, for constant love, encouragement and patience.

Christopher Hill

Introduction

'Diana, Princess of Wales, is dead' was the message in the headlines. Britain wept. The world stood still.

She would never be Queen of Great Britain, but she became Queen of British hearts. Stunned bewilderment gripped the land as grief spilled over everything.

Flowers, flowers everywhere. Flowers in the road, flowers on the gun-carriage, flowers in the park, flowers by the palace – feet thick, the sweet, haunting, tormenting perfume filling the air.

'Diana, Princess of Wales, is dead' was the message in the flowers. Britain grieved. The world watched in amazement.

Books of Memorial lay open and crammed, signatures everywhere. Crowded rooms with silent people and shuffling feet. The old, the young; men, women; the black, the white; the rich, the poor; the religious, the atheist – united in one expression of grief.

'Diana, Princess of Wales, is dead' was the message in the names.

So many messages, gift-wrapped in love and grief. Messages from the great and the good, messages from the small and the bad. Messages to comfort and encourage, messages to say, 'Thank you – we loved you – we miss you – we'll never forget you. They tell us you are dead, beloved Diana, but you will *never* die in our hearts.'

Messages behind the messages

So many messages, hundreds of thousands of them. They came from the heart. This was beyond sentiment, the collective agony of a nation ripped into by grief.

But why this degree of anguish – beyond anything seen anywhere before? The monumental mourning which greeted the death of Queen Victoria was not remotely like this. Not even heroes like King George VI commanded such a response, and on an international scale it far exceeded anything witnessed in recorded history. This was special. But why?

In answering that question we reach beyond the obvious into deep recesses in our hearts and lives. It was as if Diana *represented* us in some way. It was not only that we had lost someone dear, but also that in mourning her loss we were mourning for something far more personal – something that was a part of *us*.

Perhaps the message cards which lay alongside the flowers conveyed more than the words themselves. Did they give expression to unspoken emotions which had been stifled by 'social and political correctness'?

Triumph over tragedy

Diana had been the victim of a broken home. Victims of broken homes identified with her. One of the memories which haunted her was the sound of her mother's footsteps as she left the family home, her husband and her children. Diana was six years old. Small wonder that she was determined to be a faithful mother to her own children, come what may.

Prince Charles' affair with another man's wife, Camilla Parker Bowles, sentenced his marriage with Diana to the scrap heap from the very start. Diana fell victim to unfaithfulness and rejection from the person who had promised in his marriage vows to keep himself only for her. Even as he said the words, he knew his own duplicity. Small wonder that in her longing to be loved she eventually turned to other men. It cannot be excused but it can certainly be explained. The greater guilt does not lie with her. Victims of marital unfaithfulness and cruel rejection easily identified with Diana.

The Princess of Wales experienced many devastating life blows and yet she came through them all in tremendous style, triumphant even in her vulnerability. This gave people confidence and hope. If she could do it, so could we.

Despair over her marriage had driven her to the very edge. She had attempted suicide. She emerged as a lovely phoenix from the flames, a person from whom desperate people drew immense courage without even knowing her.

She became bulimic. Again, thousands identified with her. Obsession with her appearance and starvation of love combined to imprison her thinking, as she came to believe the lie that is bulimia. But she broke out of it and in doing so gave hope to others similarly caged.

Diana yearned for love. Prince Charles, who should have provided it but did not, even confessed publicly in a televised interview with Jonathan Dimbleby in June 1994, that he had *never* loved her and in fact had been forced into the marriage. What would be her response? Would this crushing insult finally cow her into submission and force her out of public life? That very evening Diana was due for an engagement at the Serpentine Gallery in London's Hyde Park. How would she cope? Would she even appear? Waiting photographers gasped as she burst from the limousine, a vision of loveliness in a black dress created by Christina Stambolian. She strode purposefully towards the waiting reception group and everyone knew she had once more triumphed over adversity. The rejected and unloved felt a glow of satisfaction as they looked on in genuine hope for themselves.

The loss of Diana's mother through separation and divorce had created a vacuum which was filled by her father. All through her young life he had been there, a father figure to depend upon. It was natural therefore that she would turn to him for comfort and strength in a crisis. She believed that the Royal Family and Household and the country's establishment figures were almost wholly against her, so the support of Earl Spencer was a life-saver.

Then he died. It was March 1992. Her father was not there to stand by her in her moments of deepest trauma. That year would see the publication of Andrew Morton's book *Diana: Her True Story*, a volume which tore the last vestiges of privacy from her life. Two months later the infamous 'Squidgy' tape was published, adding to her distress. Then in December, the Prime Minister, John Major, announced to a waiting world that the Prince and Princess of Wales had decided to separate. All this and no father to turn to. In this also, vast numbers of people identified with Diana. They too had found themselves deprived of a father – some through death but many through divorce or the scourge of single parenthood. Absent fathers are often little better than no fathers.

Even without the support of her devoted father, Diana came through that ghastly year. It is to her eternal credit that she did so. Once more her example served as a sign of hope – this time for those young people who face life with no father.

'Social and political correctness' lead to the mistaken view that we must 'go with the flow'. Anarchic minds apply themselves to twisting society from God's norms and there is a tendency to lie down and take it lest one be considered out of step with the trendy. We should recall the story of the Emperor's New Clothes.

Deep in the heart of many is the niggling question, 'Is this *really* the way for us to go?' Libertarian pressure groups tell us, 'Yes, it is – and we must hurtle on as fast as possible.' But the doubt remains. Is it possible that our onward rush into the so-called 'Aquarian Utopia' we are encouraged to enter is not so much a launch into orbit as a plunge into chaos?

The messages in the flowers outside Kensington Palace told of grief behind grief. We clutched at an opportunity to abandon our social and political correctness and we cried. Then we wrote – for ourselves just as much as for Diana.

Little children wrote, 'Diana, we miss you.' Perhaps they were also saying, 'Daddy, we so long to have you back. Why did you leave Mummy ... and us?'

Mothers wrote, 'Diana, we miss you.' Perhaps they were also saying, 'Dear unnamed baby I aborted, I so long to have you back. Please forgive Daddy and me for allowing you to be killed and burned.'

Young people wrote, 'Diana, we miss you.' Were they also saying, 'Dear life which I have allowed to become twisted through drugs and perversion, please come back to me made normal again'?

A new religion?

Personal grief, rejection, guilt, fear and hurt found expression in the messages of love which fluttered among the flowers. Is that why there was such an obvious *religious* dimension to what was going on? Candles burned, incense sticks smouldered away, filling the air with a pungent aroma which disturbed and soothed at the same time. It felt uncomfortable, yet strangely comforting. When people identify so closely with a hero or heroine, it is only a short step to worship. Many commentators picked up the spirit of the moment when they spoke of people making 'shrines' out of the flowers and candles. For many that is exactly what they were: places hallowed by association.

The danger of this is very clear. Veneration is not far away. Althorp Park, home of the Spencer family and Diana's final resting place, stands every chance of becoming a shrine. The mere fact that admission tickets sold by the thousand ahead of its opening to the public demonstrates that devotion to Diana has not diminished with the passing of time. Nor will it. The deep emotional carnage in the life of so many people will ensure that Diana is treated as a focus for their own sadness. The 'magic' of the Princess interred on a forbidden island in the centre of a lake adds to the mystical air of her nearness yet remoteness. It will be interesting to see if a statue of her is placed at Althorp. If so, it is certain that small replicas will begin to appear and be given prominent positions in people's homes. Idolatry has its insidious way of creeping into a nation which has abandoned clear guidelines for faith.

On BBC *Newsnight* on 8 December, it was announced that china effigies of Princess Diana were being used to adorn Christmas cribs in Portugal in place of the Virgin Mary!

We do Diana no favours if we turn her into some kind of goddess. This would actually demean her. The secret of Diana's inspiration was her *humanity*: it is this that reached out to us and found us. She truly became the 'Queen of people's hearts', in answer to her own wish.

This was her legacy. She showed us by example that the human spirit is capable of great weakness but also great strength. She showed that life's body blows need not destroy us. Her achievements are not honoured by deifying her, but rather by acknowledging her as a great human being whom we can never forget and for whom we must remain eternally grateful.

Messages from everywhere – *almost* everywhere. Messages from everyone – *almost* everyone.

Why no message from *God*?

I
'The Diana Phenomenon'

'Here is the news'

On 31 August I woke early. Maddeningly early, because I needed my sleep. But it was no good just lying there, so I slithered out of bed, brushed my teeth and crept down the stairs and out to the office. Might just as well do some work. It was around 5 am. I started a piece of work and absently turned on the radio to greet the morn. Suddenly there it was: 'Diana, Princess of Wales, together with her escort, Dodi Al Fayed ...'

The rest, as they say, is history.

There was no other news. The world had ceased to exist. All that remained was a Paris subway, a crumpled car, three dead victims of a dreadful hunt and a howling pack of *paparazzi*, snapping like crazy.

I was held in horrified, numbing suspense. I could not move. The news was awful and yet it was also fascinating. It felt like it does when I drive along the M25 and come across an accident. I want to hurry by, but somehow I want to linger ... and look. That's how it was that morning, the morning of the 31st. I remember it all so clearly.

Hour after hour the news came, scarcely changing, always insistent. 'Diana, Princess of Wales, is dead.' Announcers announced, commentators commented, experts expatiated, friends frenzied. The rest of us listened quietly as they told us for the millionth time, 'Diana, Princess of Wales, is dead.'

'Yes, I know – I heard you the first time! Can't you shut up! But no, don't shut up. I need to hear you say it for the million and first time because I cannot yet believe it. Not her. Not like this. Not ... in France.'

I could swear that those very first reports said Diana walked from the wreckage and into a waiting ambulance. Strange how the memory fades. I could swear that's what they said, but you don't find any reference to it now. 'Mortal injuries' – that's what they said later on. So I must have misheard ... I think.

That day, 31 August 1997, was my dad's birthday – he was seventy-nine years young! It's a big day in our family, a very big day.

'Buy a bunch, luv'

Was anything like this ever seen in England's green and pleasant land? A man with flowers. A woman with flowers. A yuppy with flowers. A *Big Issue* seller with flowers. A stockbroker with flowers. A Tesco girl with flowers.

'Where are you going to, my pretty maid?'

'To a great house, sir. Kensington Palace, Buckingham Palace, St James's Palace, Althorp House. I don't really mind which, just as long as they leave them be a while after I've laid them. They're lovely aren't they, the flowers?'

Reactions speak louder than words

A nation was stunned – that was certainly the first reaction. Then the nation stirred itself and there followed a period of unprecedented grief. It would be no exaggeration to say that many people displayed more open grief at the loss of Diana than they had shown at the death of close relatives. What was it about the Princess that so impressed itself upon us?

In his funeral oration her brother, Charles Spencer, spoke for all when he described her as 'the very essence of compassion, of duty, of style, of beauty ... a symbol of selfless humanity ... and a standard bearer of the rights of the downtrodden.'

Wesley Carr, Dean of Westminster, said, 'In her life, Diana profoundly influenced this nation and the world. Although a princess, she was someone for whom, from afar, we dared to feel affection and by whom we were all intrigued.' Diana impressed herself upon our hearts for many reasons.

Diana's compassion

When approached about her favourite photograph by *Le Monde*, the French newspaper, Princess Diana chose a picture of herself in a Lahore hospital cuddling a little Pakistani child stricken with cancer. As I write, that photograph is before me. Diana is pictured with her head inclined towards the child, one hand cradling it, the other grasping the child's little hand. Diana's eyes are closed as if attempting to concentrate her affection, or even in prayer. The child is scarcely able to lift its head, but the tired eyes gaze up at the extraordinary beauty embracing it.

That is how the Princess of Wales wished to be remembered – as a compassionate friend. Photographs like that continually filled our newspapers. I recall the moment in Birmingham when she swept little Laurence Chambers right off his feet. Ten year old Laurence suffers from cerebral palsy and the bear hug they shared brought a ray of unspeakable joy into both their lives.

I love the picture of her embracing an elderly victim of the conflict in Sarajevo. The old lady's frock has flowers printed all over it. Looking at that photograph now I find the flowers riveting. And what of those images of Diana reaching out and touching AIDS victims?

To some these outward demonstrations, even her journeys in the wee small hours with a cheering cup for the unfortunate night people of London, were more for the benefit of her publicity machine than for anything else. But this is unfair and in my view (for what it's worth) untrue.

No dignified distance here. She *cared*. The former Speaker of the House of Commons, George Thomas, said, 'No one ever contained so much compassion and care in one body.'

This sense of identity with the suffering masses of humanity was much more than altruism. It came of deep and dark life experiences she had endured herself which enabled her to understand, at least to some extent, the pain and sense of loss all too common in our world.

In the month of her death Diana said, 'Nothing brings me more happiness than trying to help the most vulnerable people in society. If anyone in distress calls, I will rush to them wherever I am. I touch people – it is a gesture, which comes naturally to me from the heart.'

Tony Lloyd, executive director of the Leprosy Mission, recalls trips he made with Diana which exposed her to one of the most feared of all tropical diseases. The picture that emerges is one of inspirational courage and compassion: 'She would come into a leprosy ward and within minutes people were laughing – people who hadn't laughed for years. One patient said, "This morning the sun came into our ward," following a visit from Diana.'

Pictures of her tour of Indonesia in 1989 showed her holding what was left of the hand of a leprosy victim. She was sitting on the patient's bed, looking into his face. Everyone else, it seems, kept a safe distance, gasping in admiration even as they screened themselves behind a glass partition. This was no 'photo-call'. This was raw compassion and we all loved her for it.

Diana's sense of duty

From those to whom much is given, much is expected. Diana Spencer had been given much. She was born on 1 July 1961, into the British aristocracy, the third daughter of Viscount and Viscountess Althorp and became 'Lady Diana' on the death of her grandfather, the seventh Earl Spencer.

There is something in the British heart which links privilege with duty. It is in all of us to some extent, and it flamed in the heart of Lady Diana Spencer. Her chosen career was to care for little children. Though admittedly not an academic high flyer, a lesser person in her position might well have entered one of the more flamboyant professions. But this was not Diana's way.

After a brief spell at a Swiss 'finishing school' near Gstaad (where she learned to ski) she returned to England and became nanny to a little girl in Hampshire. After this the 17 year old Diana joined a temp agency in London and took on a variety of menial jobs: cooking, cleaning and washing for various clients. Shortly after her 18th birthday, Lady Diana Spencer got what she considered to be her dream job, working as a part-timer in a Pimlico kindergarten.

Cynics might say that a girl who had failed all five of her O-levels might be expected to follow a career route like this. But that is to overlook the obvious. 'Lady Di' had connections. Qualifications or not, when it came to a career the world was her oyster, yet she chose to do the most humble things and considered them a joy. By any standard, this is remarkable.

Marriage on 29 July 1981 catapulted the now Princess of Wales into international orbit. Her royal duties began within weeks of the honeymoon. One of the first was in the Welsh town of Haverfordwest where the royal visit suffered a deluge of rain hard enough for the feathers on her hat to sag like the foliage on a weeping willow. Nothing daunted, the Princess refused to be cocooned in a raincoat because she felt the people wanted to see her. Princess Diana's natural sense of duty endeared her to the people. It appeared to be so natural for her and when combined with her innate warmth it was beguiling. She could do no wrong.

Her husband, the Prince of Wales, appeared to find her popularity increasingly tiresome, even threatening. On one memorable walkabout, when they split up to talk to the crowds on either side of a crowded street, the side that got Charles groaned quite audibly! His hurt showed clearly as he retorted, 'Sorry, you've got me. You'd better ask for your money back!'

This seemed to be an ongoing and irksome situation for the Prince, who clearly had no answer to it. It may be asked, 'Why did he need an answer?' If he truly loved his wife he would have been delighted that she was so well loved by his future subjects. But then we expose the fatal flaw in the marriage. The nation heard his own admission during the celebrated television interview with Jonathan Dimbleby in June 1994, that he was unfaithful to his wife, that he married her because he was pressured to do so and that he had never loved her.

This admission explained a good deal and certainly threw light on the Prince's inability to appreciate Diana's unassailable place in the nation's heart. He envied her because he saw her eroding his own place in the affections of the people. In so doing he failed to see that in truth Diana was his greatest asset.

The Princess's sense of duty took her beyond the call of duty. She adopted the cause of AIDS victims and in so doing showed that they were not deadly to the touch. She reached out to lepers and to so many of the untouchables of society, with a determination which soared far beyond the call of duty. It was a call of love.

Diana's style and beauty

The Princess of Wales had an infectious giggle and a sparkling sense of humour, which expressed itself in ways that revealed much about her personality. On one occasion she quipped, 'I want to be seen as a work-horse and not as a clothes-horse'! However, there is no denying that she was one of the most beautiful women in the world, and from the moment that the world knew of her relationship with Prince Charles, she became a fashion icon.

It was all very simple. Women the world over wanted to look like Diana. Since her wedding day, thousands of brides around the world have glided down the aisle, with eyes lowered, in Emanuel look-alikes. When Diana wore a fringe, fringes were 'in'; when Diana swept her hair back, the fringes disappeared.

British designers, largely unknown to the vast majority of us, became part of our national heritage: Elizabeth Emanuel, Bruce Oldfield, Zandra Rhodes. We normally indifferent British males suddenly knew the names of great continental designers like Versace, Galliano and Azagury.

The truth is, we were proud of her. Diana made us feel 'great' again, and we liked it. We liked it very much. Dazzling beauty, British made.

The seeker

Diana, Princess of Wales, had a sense of call. She was driven by her awareness that there is more to life than the world of time and space. Diana knew a need of God in her life, and she was looking for Him.

This quest was very obvious, and she shared it with so many people who have a longing for truth and solid values. Modern thinking has nudged people away from absolute to relative truth. It is the 'in thing' to say there are no absolutes. To believe in nothing is the stated wisdom of our generation and it is a total disaster. People have an innate longing for God, whether they acknowledge it or not, and Diana's seeking, expressed in the value she placed on compassion and serving others – even if she had no orthodox creed – struck deep chords in us and we wanted to identify with her.

Her quest took her along familiar paths and along strange ones. In this she followed the example of her husband, Prince Charles, whose own quest for God has led him into some surprising places. The Prince's confusion over matters religious is demonstrated by his continuing desire to be known as 'Defender of Faith' (any faith) rather than 'Defender of the (Christian) Faith'.

Diana showed a similar attitude, albeit not so vocally. Her quest took her to Calcutta and the mystical Catholicism of Mother Teresa. On the other hand Tony Lloyd, a committed evangelical Christian, recalls conversations with her: 'We had fascinating conversations about spirituality, death and hope.' Hope was a vital ingredient in Diana's life. 'There is always hope,' she would say, even in the worst leprosy ward.

Because Diana's Christian faith was not secure she was prey to deception. This showed itself in her ready acquiescence to identify with the Hindu religion and the Moslem. Her friend, Jemima Goldsmith, had married into an Islamic family and it was widely rumoured that Diana was prepared to do the same.

Princess Diana certainly dabbled with gurus, astrologers and fortune tellers, and among the last photographs taken of her were impromptu pictures taken by schoolgirls of her running from the home of her astrologer towards a waiting helicopter. Apparently none of her occult practitioners was able to foresee the tragedy which was to take place in a Paris underpass in the early hours of 31 August 1997. It is easy for them to be wise after the event. However sharp the focus of her beliefs, however defined the God she worshipped, Diana was a woman of prayer. On a particularly punishing tour of the Far East she was asked how she kept up the pace. She replied, 'It's prayer, Tony, it's prayer. I pray, not because I'm told to but because the need pours out of me.' Christopher Morgan, Religious Affairs Correspondent for the *Daily Telegraph*, wrote that a few days before Princess Diana's death she had said to a friend: 'I wish someone would teach my children how to pray.'

One major reason for the Princess's lack of religious focus must surely be the palpable failure of Church leaders in Britain to make the gospel plain. Royals are no different from anyone else when it comes to understanding the truth about Christ. If they are fed a diet of doubt and compromise by those who are supposed to be 'shepherds to the flock' it is small wonder that they are fair game for deception. If those who attempt to lead the blind are themselves self-blinded, tragedy is the only consequence. Diana, Princess of Wales, was one of thousands of casualties resulting from this appalling failure on the part of so-called 'Guardians of the Faith'.

The sincerity of Diana's seeking should not be questioned. She sought answers and was ready to go to great lengths to find them. From the writer's perspective it is the deepest tragedy that she often sought them in the wrong places and may have missed out on the one certainty in all of this:

> Jesus Christ is the Way, the Truth and the Life, and no one comes to the Father except through Him (compare John 14:6).

2
What Did the Diana Prophecy Say?

It was a British Sunday in late summer: 31 August 1997, a Sunday in prospect much like any other. But this Sunday was to go into history as a 'day of rest' which brought stillness to the whole nation and to vast areas of the world.

In the middle of the morning a woman stood up in a Sheffield church. Walkley Baptist Church was about to be put on the map.

'I believe God has spoken to me ... '

The congregation was riveted.

One Friday in May, Ginny Burgin, Sheffield housewife and mother of two, received a strong impression that God was speaking to her. She had been a Christian for a number of years and was well aware that God speaks to people – usually through the Bible or through preachers. But this was different. She was convinced God was speaking to her personally and directly. It wasn't so much a voice, more an impression. But it was very strong.

It had happened several times before, but not like this. This was something special. Ginny knew that from the moment it started.

I am at work in the heart and spirit of the people of this nation. I am doing a work which at the moment is very, very unseen. But it is happening quicker than you think. Things are happening much more quickly than you think. And as a sign – this shall be a sign – that *there will be a day very soon when the whole nation will mourn: and the whole nation will put flowers in their cities.*

Ginny was not sure what to make of this. What could it mean? What event could bring mourning to the whole nation? It would need to be a person of great prominence, someone deeply loved by all. Could it be the Queen Mother? She certainly hoped not. Ginny was not sure what to do.

She consulted the leaders of Walkley Baptist, her local church, and was advised to keep the 'message' to herself for the time being. The leaders felt God might add to what had been given as she continued to pray, and even show her how, when and where it should be made public.

On Sunday 31 August, Ginny was preparing to go to church for the morning service when her husband came in and announced that he had heard some very bad news. Princess Diana had been killed in a car crash on a Paris street. As soon as she heard the news, Ginny knew this was the national tragedy to which the 'message' referred. She had received it on 16 May, over three months before the event.

When she arrived at church, the congregation was buzzing with the tragic news. Ginny knew she must make public what she truly believed God had said to her. The leaders agreed that she should do so. As she began to speak, Ginny became aware that the 'message' was being extended. When she came to the end of what had been given her on 16 May, she continued,

When that day happens the sign is this: the speed at which the heart and the spirit of the people of this nation can be affected, that is the speed at which I will work among this nation. Do not think that what you see and hear of are small insignificant happenings. Do not despise the day of small things. For I tell you, when you see this sign, I am on the move, says the Lord. And I am on the move in the cities of this nation and where flowers are laid my Spirit will be moving faster than those flowers are removed.

For I am bringing the power of my Spirit to bear on the cities of this nation. And as fast as that mourning went through the nation, joy will go through this nation. And I tell you, says the Lord, that you will know the miraculous entering your lives. I tell you that you will see changes in areas where you never expected to see changes. You will see relatives who you never expected to see coming into the Kingdom of God. You will know areas in your life where you've battled and battled and never overcome – and you will overcome in a day, says the Lord. For I am at work in this nation and I will bring this nation to its knees before me and they will know the joy of their salvation in the mighty risen Lord Jesus.

Therefore rejoice. And do not let that spirit of mourning grasp at your hearts. Therefore let the rivers of living water flow from within you and know that you will have many opportunities from this point to

speak of my grace, to speak of my love, to see in action
my Spirit at work. Know that I will be with you in
that and you will see the miraculous, says the Lord.

It is important to remember that at that morning service
on the very day of Diana's death there was no hint of the
deluge of flowers that would pour from the nation's grief.

As may be imagined, this 'message', once supported
by the leaders of Walkley Baptist Church, was flashed
round the churches in record time. It was not long before
Christians (chiefly from the Charismatic constituency)
from Land's End to John O'Groats had heard about it. It
spread like wild-fire.

In spite of its lack of grammatical precision, it was
immediately hailed as a word from God – a 'prophecy' – by
those who wished to underwrite its divine origin. A roller-
coaster of interpretation and expectation was set in
motion and it began to hurtle down the track.

The 'prophecy' remained (and remains) unheard of in
many of the more traditional churches, but within many
charismatic churches it was spread around with enthusiasm. It was seen as a harbinger of impending spiritual
revival and raised the hopes of many Christians who over
recent years have been encouraged to expect what they
conceive as an imminent 'move of God'.

3
What is Prophecy?

In the letter to the Hebrews, the writer makes a clear comment on the purpose of Old Testament prophecy. Chapter 1, verse 1 reads: 'In the past *God spoke* to our forefathers *through the prophets at many times, and in various ways.'*

This simple definition is repeated in a variety of forms and in different parts of the Bible. For example, '... you must understand that no prophecy of Scripture came about by the prophet's own interpretation. For *prophecy never had its origin in the will of man, but men spoke from God as they were carried along by the Holy Spirit'* (2 Peter 1:20–21).

So Old Testament prophets had an amazing authority and responsibility. They were able to speak and write words which had come straight from the mind of God. When they said 'Thus saith the Lord ...', that's the way it was. They were writing Scripture – God's Word. It was the eternal Word of God set in time and space by inspiration of the Holy Spirit through the minds of certain chosen men. So to disobey or disregard the words of a true prophet was to scorn God Himself.

Interestingly, when we turn to the New Testament we discover another set of men who wrote Scripture. Peter

refers to one such in his second letter, chapter 3, verse 16:
'[Paul's] letters contain some things that are hard to understand, which ignorant and unstable people distort, as they
do the *other Scriptures*, to their own destruction.'

We could wonder if Peter's use of the word 'Scripture'
is somehow different from, say, Matthew 22:29, where the
word clearly refers to the Old Testament Scriptures. But
linguistically there would be no possible justification for
doing this. Arndt and Gingrich in their monumental
Greek-English Lexicon of the New Testament (University of
Chicago Press, 1973, p. 165) state that the Greek word
'*graphe*' is used'... in the New Testament *exclusively* with a
sacred meaning of *Holy Scripture*'.

So there can be no reasonable doubt that Peter considered Paul's letters to be equal in authority to the Old
Testament. A simply extraordinary claim for one Jew to
make of another living Jew several hundred years after the
closing of the Old Testament literature with the Book
of Malachi.

It is fascinating to note that in contrast with the Old
Testament writers, New Testament Scripture writers are
never called 'prophets'. They are called 'apostles'. The
apostles emerge as the New Testament counterparts of
the Old Testament prophets, having inspiration and
authority to write Scripture.

According to Wayne Grudem (*Systematic Theology*,
Zondervan, 1994, p. 1050) the Hebrew word *nabi* (prophet) meant 'one who speaks God's very words', but there
is a major difference between the Old Testament prophet
and the New. The Greek *prophetes* at the time of the New
Testament had a broad range of meanings, but generally
had the sense of 'one who speaks on the basis of some

external influence' (often a spiritual influence of some kind, but not always).

Paul refers in Titus 1:12 to Epimenides, a pagan Greek poet, as a prophet. Clearly there could be nothing of a truly divine origin in what Epimenides prophesied. Whatever external influence motivated him it was not the Holy Spirit.

In his article on the word 'prophet' in the *Theological Dictionary of the New Testament* (ed. G. Kittel, Eerdmans, 1964–74, vol. 6, p. 794) Helmut Kramer concludes that the Greek word *prophetes* 'simply expresses the formal function of "declaring, proclaiming, making known". Yet, because every prophet declares something which is not his own, the Greek word for "herald" (*keryx*) is the closest synonym.'

Wayne Grudem concludes that the word 'prophet' was used in the New Testament of ordinary Christians who spoke simply to report something that God had lain on their hearts or brought to their minds. The New Testament makes it clear that, although very important for building up the Church, the gift of prophecy had less authority than the Bible had, and even less than that of recognized Bible teachers.

These quotations should be sufficient to show that the greatest caution needs to be exercised before allowing a 'prophecy' to dictate. Tests need to be applied to it with love and encouragement, but also with firmness and rigour.

It is very significant that nowhere in the New Testament are Christians encouraged to listen to contemporary prophets for Church direction, but are *always* pointed to the Scriptures. The great apostles Paul and Peter make it crystal clear. In 2 Timothy 2:15, Paul urges his friend, 'Do your best to present yourself to God as one approved, a workman ... who correctly handles the word of truth.'

In the same letter, 3:16, Paul says, 'All Scripture is God-breathed and is useful for doctrine, rebuking, correcting and training in righteousness, so that the man of God may be thoroughly equipped for every good work.'

Peter in his second letter, 1:19–21, encourages his readers to 'pay attention' to Scripture which he describes as 'a lamp shining in a dark place'.

We know that there were many prophets ministering at the time, but we find the apostles consistently urging us to live by the Scriptures and not by the ministrations of prophets in the churches. So what is the place of prophecy today?

Although prophecies are the spontaneous promptings of the Holy Spirit which He brings to the minds of Christians, they should not automatically be given the status of the words of God. An impression that God is wanting to make His will known, highlighting a Scripture passage, addressing a specific situation in the affairs of the church – such are the great values of prophetic words. But they are only ever what the Christian is led to say. Discernment is required in the Church to know who or what has led the person to speak. Is it God, is it the prophet's own wishful thinking or has it some malevolent source?

The authority of prophecy is less than the authority of teaching the Bible. This is different from the impression given in some quarters where prophets are seen as the most important leaders in the Church. The fact is, it was teachers, not prophets, who gave leadership and direction in the early Church. Prophecy is always to be exercised under the authority of the written Word – the responsibility of Bible teachers. So we may say that prophecies in the Church today are not the words of God, they are the words of men, though at their best they are saturated in the Word of God.

In the light of this, we may see how valuable prophecy is in the life of a church, and why Paul is so enthusiastic about the genuine article. But it is not helpful when those who present prophecies to the local church for testing insist on prefacing their message with 'Thus saith the Lord'. It invests the message with an infallibility which is misleading and discourages proper examination.

Donald Bridge in his book *Signs and Wonders Today* (IVP, 1985, p. 183) says,

> The illuminist constantly finds that 'God tells him' to do things ... Illuminists are often very sincere, very dedicated, and possessed of a commitment to obey God that shames more cautious Christians. Nevertheless they are treading a dangerous path. Their ancestors have trodden it before, and always with disastrous results in the long run. Inner feelings and special promptings are by their very nature subjective. *The Bible provides our objective guide.*

Paul is extremely encouraging to prophets in the Church. He wants to see the ministry flourishing. The reason for this is made clear in 1 Corinthians 14:3: 'everyone who prophesies speaks to men for their strengthening, encouragement and comfort'.

When they are truly inspired by God, they are tremendous blessings to God's people. No wonder Paul enthuses about prophecy! It is because of the importance of this gift that we need to treat it in a responsible manner.

The gift of prophecy in the Church is available to all Christians, not just those who are teachers or skilled speakers. When Peter preached on the Day of Pentecost he quoted from the prophecy of Joel and said, 'Your sons and your daughters will prophesy, your young men will see visions, your old men will dream dreams. Even on my servants, both men and women, I will pour out my Spirit in those days, and they will prophesy' (Acts 2:17–18).

When Paul wrote to the Church at Corinth he said that he wanted all the Christians to prophesy (1 Corinthians 14:5) and he said, 'For you can all prophesy in turn so that everyone may be instructed and educated' (1 Corinthians 14:31). Writing to the congregation in general Paul said, 'Follow the way of love and eagerly desire spiritual gifts, especially the gift of prophecy' (1 Corinthians 14:1).

What about foretelling the future?

There is a common misconception that prophecy is forecasting the future. But even the great prophets in the Old Testament only rarely foretold coming events. This was not their main emphasis, although clearly their ministry included the foretelling of certain key events.

The prophet Isaiah wrote, 'A virgin will be with child and will give birth to a son, and will call Him Immanuel' (Isaiah 7:14). Matthew quotes it in his Gospel (1:23) as foretelling the birth of Jesus 700 years later.

The prophet Micah said the Messiah would be born in Bethlehem (Micah 5:2). Zechariah foretold His riding into Jerusalem as King on Palm Sunday (Zechariah 9:9).

Isaiah wrote, 'He was led like a lamb to the slaughter, and as a sheep before her shearers is silent, so he did not open his mouth ... he was cut off from the land of the living; for the transgression of my people he was stricken' (Isaiah 53:7, 8). This is quoted in Acts 8:32–35, where Philip clearly links it with the death of Jesus.

While it is true that there are many passages in the Old Testament which foretell future events in the life of Israel and Judah and also predict detailed moments in the life of Jesus, we must remember that the primary function of the prophet was to convey the word, will and heart of God to His people. Prophets were motivated by a driving compulsion to apply God's Law and act as guardians of the Covenant.

In the New Testament also the primary emphasis is on relating the Word of God to the needs of His people. The relationship between Scripture and prophecy is very obvious. Predictive elements are certainly there, however. In Acts 11:28 we are introduced to a prophet named Agabus. Through the Spirit Agabus 'predicted that a severe famine would spread over the entire Roman world'.

The writer of Acts (Luke) immediately comments, 'This happened during the reign of Claudius'. The effect of this prophecy was that the disciples in Antioch decided to provide help for their fellow believers in Judaea. Clearly they took the prophecy as a revelation inspired by the Holy Spirit and then acted on it.

The example given by Luke in Acts 21:10–14 shows that such prophecies were not always treated as divine revelation even when they were given by the same prophet. Agabus came down to the Roman harbour city of

Caesarea and had a personal word of prophecy for Paul. 'Coming over to us he took Paul's belt, tied his own hands and feet with it and said, "The Holy Spirit says, 'In this way the Jews of Jerusalem will bind the owner of this belt and will hand him over to the Gentiles'."'

The reaction of Paul is quite different from that of his friends. They immediately took this prophecy as being authentic and a dire warning of dark deeds in Jerusalem. They pleaded with him not even to go to Jerusalem. Paul's reaction was to reject the prophecy. Had it been genuinely inspired by the Holy Spirit, Paul would certainly have acknowledged it and acted accordingly, but he did not. Clearly the prophecy was not genuine. Its source was either in Agabus' good intentions or else it was inspired by other spiritual forces. Either way Paul rejected it.

The fact that Agabus was prophesying falsely is confirmed in that what he said did not happen. Agabus said Paul would be bound by the *Jews* who would then hand him over to the Gentiles (presumably the Romans). A close reading of Acts shows that although arrested in Jerusalem, Paul was not bound by the Jews nor did they hand him over to the Romans. He was *rescued* from the Jews by the Romans for his own safety. The Jews had no desire for this, they wanted to deal with Paul in their own way. The involvement of the Romans was not at the instigation of the Jews – quite the opposite. Furthermore, the Jews did not bind Paul, the Romans did (verse 33).

So the revelation which Agabus claimed to have was seriously flawed. Paul clearly sensed this and rejected the prophecy. If the prophecy came from Agabus's own thinking we can recognize a genuine, though misguided concern for his brother Paul. If the source was from some occult powers, we can see that the intention was to deflect Paul from God's clear purpose. Either way, the need to discern truth from error was vital.

Applying the tests

From all that has been said, there are various tests which we should apply to any prophecy in the Church today. This list of questions is not necessarily given in order of priority, but it seems to the writer that these are the ones which should be asked. Other writers may have different tests, but these would seem to be sufficient for the purpose.

Is the person giving this prophecy a truly committed Christian?

True prophecy in the New Testament Church was expected and received through Christians. The reason for this is obvious. Prophecy is a gift of the Holy Spirit, and only Christians can receive the gifts. They are given for the exercise of Christ's ministry in the world through His Church.

Other people of different faiths and none also claim to have 'prophetic gifts' of one kind and another. We must not dismiss them all out of hand as being tricksters. Many are totally genuine in their belief and practice. But the great question is, what is the *source* of this revelation?

It is only true believers – those who trust in Jesus Christ as Lord and Saviour – who can receive the Holy Spirit: and only Holy Spirit-filled believers who can prophesy in Christ's name and with His authority.

Is the person's life in order and well endorsed by the local church leadership?

We cannot expect the Holy Spirit to give revelation to people who are not living right. This is not a cry for perfection, but it is a call for common sense. If a Christian is living by standards which are less than Christian, he can scarcely command confidence in other believers if he comes out with a statement he suggests has come by inspiration of God!

We should hesitate before accepting as prophetic any so-called revelation which is given by a person who is not endorsed by the leaders of the congregation as being in a healthy spiritual state. If there are major personality problems or worldly attitudes, the leaders should know about it and treat forthcoming prophecies with great caution before releasing them on a congregation.

Is the content of the prophecy consistent with Bible truth or is some part of it questionable on biblical grounds?

If any part of a prophetic statement is shown to be unbiblical it must be rejected out of hand. The inspirer of true prophecy is the Holy Spirit of *Truth* (John 14:17; 16:13), and that is *God's* Truth – the Truth of God's Word.

That is not to say that a prophetic revelation must always comprise pure Scripture, or even contain some, but it is impossible for something of divine origin to be inconsistent with Scripture.

Is the content of the prophecy the sort of thing the person is known for?

It is all too easy for a person to project their own pet ideas and cherished opinions into prophetic form! The wish can become father to the prophecy! This is not to say that we should necessarily dismiss some impassioned encouragement to pray when such is given by a known intercessor, but it certainly calls into question, 'The Lord is saying, "The choir stalls are an abomination to Me!"', when the 'prophet' has been petitioning the church council for years to get the choir stalls out!

Is the prophecy being used to get at some member or group in the congregation?

If a prophetic form is being used to make a personal attack or comment upon people it is highly unlikely to be genuine. The overall effect of true prophecy is to build up, not to tear down.

Is the prophecy meeting the criteria of I Corinthians 14:3, namely strengthening, encouragement and comfort?

Paul is very enthusiastic about prophesying in the Church. It is a wonderful God-given means of building up Christians in their faith. But he explains very clearly the effect of such revelations. They will not be trivial, they will have a very powerful effect. The three words Paul uses to describe their effect are 'strengthening, encouragement and comfort'.

The word 'strengthening' is the Greek, *oikodome*, which means 'build, construct, make very strong'. 'Encouragement' is *paraklesis*, 'call alongside for help, encouragement'. It is an enormously important New Testament word and Jesus uses the noun form to describe the Holy Spirit. He is the *Parakletos* (John 14:16, 26; 15:26; 16:7). 'Comfort' is *paramuthia*, meaning 'consolation'.

These are powerful terms and serve to demonstrate

the crucial importance of encouraging the ministry of true prophecy in the Church. It serves to build up the congregation, making it strong to withstand spiritual attack.

Have others weighed what has been prophesied and given their support, according to I Corinthians 14:29?

Because of its great importance to the well-being of a congregation, prophecy must be weighed and tested by the local church. There are various passages in the New Testament which make it clear that *all* church members may prophesy, so presumably it is the whole congregation which needs to weigh a prophecy which has been given.

Once this is done the prophecy can be applied in ways indicated within it. How should we respond? What have we to believe? What have we to do? If the process of testing the prophecy does not lead to some kind of change for the better in the life of the congregation it is highly likely that the prophecy was not divinely inspired in the first place.

If it has a predictive element to it, has it come true?

One of the scandals of the Church is the way in which people are permitted to make outlandish statements under the guise of 'prophecy', and when they are found to be untrue the whole matter is conveniently forgotten! No apology is made, nor any attempt to rectify the situation. Sadly, this has often happened at the highest levels of leadership within the Charismatic churches, and ministers with great reputations are allowed to 'get away with it'.

Confident predictions of Revival are commonplace, even with specific dates! One American preacher confidently prophesied that Jesus would return for the Church (the Rapture) on 14 May 1997. His books were distributed by the thousand all over the world. It did not happen, so he has suggested another date!

American pulpiteers vie with their British counterparts to tell the world that Revival is just around the corner. Everyone gets excited because the great 'guru' hath spoken! Nothing happens. What then? Is the prophet held to account for misleading the people? Never! He is always allowed to slither out of his responsibility and to prepare himself for his next outlandish prediction. Are the people incredulous this time? No, not at all – they urge him on! If it were not so tragic, it would be laughable.

Are all parts of the prophecy equally authentic?

In 1 Corinthians 13:9 Paul says that 'we prophesy in part'. He says that there will be imperfections in our prophesying. By this he clearly does not mean glaring errors, but rather minor imperfections. Getting dates wrong could scarcely be included in such imperfections!

One of my friends is a highly experienced Elim Pastor in London's East End. He has heard many prophecies through the years, and has some strange tales to tell! His experience shows that even with the best of prophecies – those with a high degree of inspiration – there is usually 'four penn'orth' which is the speaker's own contribution. This has to be identified and discarded.

Is the prophecy glorifying Jesus Christ?

According to John 16:14, Jesus says that the Holy Spirit 'will bring glory to Me'. This is borne out by many New Testament passages. Everything the Holy Spirit says and does glorifies Jesus Christ. This provides us with a vital piece of evidence when evaluating a prophecy. Does this prophecy glorify Jesus Christ? It does not mean that He is always named in a prophecy, but is the overall effect to glorify Him?

If it glorifies someone else, it is clearly a false prophecy. Its subject can be the Church, the world, individual believers, great events, but the overall effect of the prophecy should be to glorify Jesus Christ. This is always the goal of the Holy Spirit, and is His authenticating mark.

Is the prophecy cutting across what has been taught from the Bible by introducing a completely new idea?

If a prophecy is given after the preaching of God's Word, it should serve that message and not act as a diversion from it. The reason for this is that the Bible is always superior to prophecy. The Scripture is the Word of God in a way that prophecy in the Church today could never be. It is a different level of revelation.

Sometimes a prophecy will be given at the conclusion of a Bible exposition which sets it alight and punches the message across. This is prophecy at its best. There are other occasions, however, when a 'prophetic word' given at the end of a sermon all but destroys the impact of the Bible exposition by drawing people's attention away from it. This is disastrous but, sadly, all too common.

A great friend of mine is a world renowned preacher. He was preaching in a mainline church quite recently, and had delivered the Word of the Lord faithfully and well. It had taken him many hours to prepare his sermon, and he sensed the power of God upon him as he preached. Being a guest preacher, he was permitted to preach for an hour and he did so.

At the end of his sermon, the minister thanked my friend for his wonderful address and then turned to the large congregation and said they would now wait to see if there would be 'a word from the Lord'! Understandably my friend was rather disturbed by the implication, thinking to himself, 'What on earth does he think I've been bringing to the people over the last hour?'

A silence followed, broken eventually by a member of the congregation who stood and said the Lord had given her a prophecy. 'I see a lot of people riding bicycles, but the bicycles have no chains.'

The 'prophet' sat down, admitting to the assembled parishioners that she had not the slightest idea what it could mean. Without commenting on the 'revelation', the minister invited further contributions. They came, and were equally inane.

My friend, now in a state of almost overwhelming agitation, rose from his place and went to the microphone. The congregation sat on edge, clearly anticipating the great man's interpretation of these supposed prophecies. But instead he said into the microphone, 'For God's sake, go home!'

That probably *was* the word of the Lord! They left. He left, and has not been invited back!

An interesting sequel to this story is that a number of people attending the service were so challenged by my friend's interjection, and confronted by their own gullibility in accepting the pseudo-prophecy in such an uncritical manner, that they met for prayer and prayed through until 4.30 the following morning!

4
Testing the Diana Prophecy

Some interesting coincidences?

Many Christians up and down the land have hailed the 'Diana Prophecy' as a definite word from God.

The original statement – Part One of the 'prophecy' – was received by Ginny Burgin on Friday 16 May 1997, two days before the Jewish festival of Pentecost. This festival commemorates the giving of the Law to Israel at Mount Sinai, around 1500 BC. Pentecost is also celebrated by Christians and commemorates the coming of the Holy Spirit to the disciples of Jesus in 33 AD. To some this helped to confirm that the first part of the 'Diana Prophecy' had God's stamp of approval.

The date also coincided with the 'March for Jesus' event, which saw thousands of Christians walking in procession through town and city streets all over Britain, praying for a spiritual revival as they walked. There were at least 750 such marches taking place between 16 and 18 May. It is suggested by some that the 'Diana Prophecy' was a divine response to the prayers of the marchers.

Charismatic Church leader, Gerald Coates, also points out that several thousand Christians nationwide had been

fasting and praying for revival over a 40-day period, cul-
minating in the feast of Pentecost, 18 May. Could it be that
God was responding to this?

Like the curate's egg?

The proverbial curate's egg was good in parts. Paul the
apostle appears to say much the same thing with respect
to prophecy. In his first letter to the Church in Corinth he
wrote, 'For we know in part and we prophesy in part'
(1 Corinthians 13:9).

Paul was also insistent that all who claim to prophesy
must submit their revelations to scrupulous testing before
they can be acknowledged as genuine. So as far as Paul
was concerned, we should not accept at face value everything that is said to be prophetic.

It is perfectly clear that the 'Diana Prophecy' is in two
parts; the first given on 16 May, the second and longer
part on 31 August. Why would God separate such a message in this way? Is it in two parts for a reason? Is the first
part more authentic than the second, or vice versa? How
can we be sure that *any* of it is authentic? Is the entire
'prophecy' to be taken or left, or may we say that certain
parts are genuinely from God and other parts not? Such
questions are very important and we must now turn to an
examination of them.

Applying the tests

When Paul was preaching in the Macedonian town of Berea (Acts 17:10–12), during his second apostolic journey, his preaching in the local synagogue was treated with a good deal of caution. The Berean Jews did not simply sit there with mouths gaping, drinking in every word as if it had come down from heaven. Luke, the author of Acts, says, 'Now the Bereans ... received the message with great eagerness and examined the Scriptures every day to see if what Paul said was true.'

At first sight this may appear extremely insulting. Imagine checking out the preaching of such an illustrious visitor as Paul! But Luke, far from indicating that they were out of order in doing what they did, commends the Bereans for it and describes them as being more noble than their neighbours in Thessalonica. When Paul preached in that town, the Jews simply reacted to his message without checking to see if it had biblical authority.

The message was no less shocking to the Berean Jews, but they gave Paul the respect his courage deserved and searched the Old Testament to make sure his preaching was 'kosher'. It was! Luke reports in Acts 17:12 that 'Many of the Jews believed, as did also a number of prominent Greek women and many Greek men.'

So, seeking to authenticate a 'word from God' is not a negative reaction, but an extremely positive one because it shows we are taking the whole thing very seriously and treating the speaker with maximum respect.

Speaking as a preacher, it is always an encouragement to me when members of the congregation are following my preaching in their Bibles and taking notes. And even more so when they write to me with questions. This shows a caring and responsible attitude to me and to my preaching which only serves to clarify what God is saying. I never treat it as being impertinent and critical. I am always very grateful for it, even when I do not agree!

This is the reason why I have a group of people who support my work by providing checks and balances. If any one of them has reason to question my teaching or behaviour, there is total freedom to speak without fear of losing my friendship! Those who dare to speak the Word of God *must* be accountable, and be *seen* to be accountable.

The same principle applies to prophecy in the Church. If the prophet is not prepared to have his or her word scrutinized by those meant to receive it, that person forfeits the right to be taken seriously. We need to apply these tests to the 'Diana Prophecy'. This is not to cast aspersions on Ginny Burgin, the woman who received it. On the contrary, it is to treat her with appropriate respect.

People in Israel often joke and say, 'Two Jews, three opinions!' It is no less a joke among Christians. Two Christians, three opinions! This is certainly exemplified in the reactions of Christians to the 'Diana Prophecy'. Some embraced it like a life raft, seeing it as justification for their hopes of impending spiritual revival. Others dismissed it out of hand as being little more than wishful thinking or maybe as even coming from an occult source! The more difficult course – but probably the wisest – is to say that it may well be genuine prophecy *in part*. As with every prophecy the need for true discernment lies in picking out the true from the false and avoiding the temptation to read things into it which we want to see there. What is it *actually* saying? And what does it mean?

Is the person giving this prophecy a truly committed Christian: a person whose life is in order and well endorsed by the local church leadership?

The leaders of Walkley Baptist Church in Sheffield speak warmly of Ginny Burgin and believe her life to be consistent with her Christian profession. On 8 December Ray Booth, Pastor of Walkley Baptist Church, publicly stated on BBC Television *Newsnight* that 'It was a word from God that a significant event would take place that would move the nation. I would feel that this prophecy has ... been weighed by many churches ...'

Is the content of the prophecy consistent with Bible truth or is some part of it questionable on biblical grounds?

There is nothing in the 'Diana Prophecy' which could be described as inconsistent with or contrary to Scripture, unless we insist upon saying that it clearly states that spiritual revival is a feature of the days immediately before the Return of Jesus. If that is indeed the message in the 'prophecy' we have a problem, because nowhere does the Bible say that. On the contrary there is a large amount of teaching that *tribulation* will mark the Last Days, and Christians need to prepare for it.

Part Two includes a quotation from the Old Testament prophecy of Zechariah. Chapter 4:10 asks, 'Who despises the day of small things?' The Bible context of this question is the rebuilding of the ruined Temple of Solomon by the Jews who returned from Babylon. It was a shadow of the former structure, but in the event it served the people just as well and actually lasted longer.

The clear emphasis here is a warning not to look for the spectacular, but rather to trust that the Lord is active in people's lives even though we cannot see much obvious evidence of it.

Is the content of the prophecy the sort of thing the person is known for?

Whilst it would be true to say that Ginny Burgin belongs to a church which encourages prophecies, and that on her own admission on BBC *Newsnight* she is given to seeing 'pictures' in her mind, it would be untrue to say that she had the idea of flowers in the cities before the 'prophecy' came.

When she received the 'prophecy' her first reaction was to think that the day of mourning and flower laying must apply to the Queen Mother, who being elderly might be expected to die in the near future. So the reference to flowers in the cities was not suggestive of anything connected with Diana, Princess of Wales. It did not come into *anyone's* thinking.

Is the prophecy being used to get at some member or group in the congregation?

Clearly not!

Is the prophecy meeting the criteria of 1 Corinthians 14:3, namely strengthening, encouragement and comfort?

In the BBC *Newsnight* programme on 8 December 1997, Pastor Ray Booth stated, 'I would feel that this prophecy ... falls into the biblical criteria of strengthening the saints of God, encouraging them and bringing them comfort.'

From this we may deduce that Pastor Booth is convinced of the veracity of the prophecy and that it has had a very positive impact upon Walkley Baptist Church, strengthening, encouraging and bringing comfort to members of the congregation.

Other Charismatic leaders like Roger Forster and Gerald Coates were quick to endorse the prophecy for its tremendous encouragement and the groups of churches they represent, Ichthus and Pioneer, have followed suit. The same could be said for many other Charismatic churches, both outside recognized denominations and within them.

The tenor of the 'Diana Prophecy' is decidedly upbeat, speaking of God moving quickly to bring the power of His Spirit to bear on the cities of Britain. The effect of this miraculous intervention will include unexpected changes for the good within families, with formerly hardened relatives suddenly coming into the Kingdom of God. It will bring sudden victory to Christians who have battled in particular areas of life over many years without seeing a breakthrough. The prophecy predicts that Britain will be brought to its knees before God, which could mean revival leading to worship or else judgement leading to cries of mercy. Either way, joy in the risen Jesus Christ is forecast as the wonderful end in prospect.

This is no time for a spirit of mourning to grasp at Christians' hearts: many opportunities to speak to people of God's grace and love will come and the Church will know God's presence and see His Spirit at work in miraculous ways. If all this is truly a message from God, it is no wonder that many Christians have felt strengthened, encouraged and comforted by it.

**Have others weighed what has been prophesied and
given their support according to 1 Corinthians 14:29?**

Pastor Ray Booth said publicly that the prophecy had been
weighed by *many* churches. We do not know which
churches he means, nor do we know what tests were
applied.

Walkley Baptist Church is associated with a group of
Charismatic churches within New Frontiers International,
which is led by Terry Virgo and his team. It is likely that the
churches referred to by Pastor Booth are those with which
he already has a close relationship. There was certainly no
opportunity given to other Sheffield churches to weigh
the prophecy before releasing it. This is a pity, because
it would have added hugely to the credibility of the
prophecy if a significant number of local Sheffield
churches had endorsed it before release.

When prophetic statements are made, those who
accept them as genuine need to be convinced in their
own minds. Simply because Mrs Burgin's local pastor
considers the 'Diana Prophecy' to be well judged and
authentic, it does not follow that we should follow suit.
Each of us is responsible before the Lord for our own
actions and that includes responding to prophecies. If for
whatever reason we have hesitations, we must acknowledge them and proceed with the greatest caution, or not
proceed at all.

If it has a predictive element within it, has it come true?

Here we are again confronted by the proverbial curate's
egg – it's good in parts! There are elements within the
'Diana Prophecy' which are truly remarkable. Part One,
delivered on 16 May, is startling in its prediction that a

coming national event would result in huge numbers putting flowers in their cities.

In the BBC *Newsnight* programme previously referred to, Cristina Odone, described as an 'author and critic', was engaged as an expert contributor. Her contribution showed a surprising lack of research when she announced, 'The prophecy that there will be a nation united in grief and flowers strewn over the land – certainly that could have been applied to Dunblane. It could have been applied to a number of other national events, national tragedies. So I fear that even at this level we can take it with a pinch of salt.'

The first part of the prophecy was given in May 1997 – a long time *after* the tragic massacre at Dunblane. As to the 'other national events, national tragedies' referred to, I must confess that apart from Diana's death I have no recollection of any tragic, national event in 1997 at which vast numbers of flowers were laid in our cities.

By any standards Part One of the prophecy is remarkable. It says that the laying of the flowers would be a *sign* that God is at work in the heart and spirit of our people – no more, no less.

Suppose it is true. What does it mean? At the very least it means that as a result of Diana's death Christians have a unique opportunity for evangelism. Part Two of the prophecy lays nearly all the emphasis upon *God* working in the nation, almost independent of His Church. But in the final paragraph there is a further great encouragement to seize our opportunities to speak about God's grace and love and to witness the Holy Spirit in action.

The death of Diana, Princess of Wales, has certainly created an openness to discuss spiritual things. On 1

September, the day after the Paris tragedy, a remarkable book called *The Final Frontier* (ed. Richard Kent and Val Fotherby, Marshall Pickering, 1997) was published. The timing of its release was extraordinary. The book is a collection of short accounts of 'near death experiences'. It was thoroughly researched by Dr Kent (a Christian medical doctor with many years' experience) and deals with the stark choice which faces every person: where will we spend eternity – in heaven or in hell? The book has sold in record numbers and is bought particularly by non-Christians. Many people have come to faith in Christ through reading the book. Another coincidence? I do not believe so.

If the prophecy achieves nothing else, it should certainly make *all* Christians wake up to the vast opportunity presented to us in the death of Diana. Never mind if we are Charismatic, non-Charismatic, New Church, Old Church, Black Church, White Church ... even *Green* Church! People are desperate to know what will happen to them when they die. How can we sell them short?

Does this mean I am suggesting that the entire 'Diana Prophecy' is to be treated as true prophecy? I answer, no. Some of its predictions are not true.

It is the element of speed which troubles me most. Many Charismatic preachers are encouraging people to look for a soon-coming revival. The emphasis is on *now* and *just around the corner*. People are praying for it, fasting for it, singing for it, dancing for it ... and travelling long distances to get a touch of it. But the fact is, it has not come. People get disillusioned when their hopes are deferred. So apparent interventions from God are most welcome!

Enthusiasts look for encouragements wherever they may be found and the 'Diana Prophecy' has provided a supreme one. It was confidently anticipated by Gerald Coates that the six weeks it took for the flowers to be cleared meant that a significant spiritual movement would be let loose in London and in other parts of the country well before the end of 1997. This arose from the statement in the prophecy, 'And I am on the move in the cities of this nation and where flowers are laid *My Spirit will be moving faster than those flowers are removed.*'

Gerald is a man with an enormous capacity to love people, and I know of few others who can inspire Christians to get involved in society as he does, but in regard to the 'Diana Prophecy', if Gerald's interpretation of the prophecy is right, the prophecy is not correct. But perhaps Gerald's interpretation is not true. We cannot have it both ways. One thing is for certain, the expected outpouring has not taken place.

The element of speed also affects the way God is expected to sweep joy through the nation, to bring unexpected changes, conversions, personal victories and so forth. Because we live in an 'instant' society, where everything must be provided as quickly as possible, such talk of instant blessing is very exciting and appealing, but it appears to run counter to the way things are actually going.

The 'Diana Prophecy' is clearly a mixture. But here we must be very careful. Christians have an alarming tendency to swing to extremes. Some Christians insist that the whole prophecy is 'from the Lord', others that none of it is! If I say that some of the prophecy is in my view quite genuine, I shall be written off by some of my more conservative friends as having gone soft. On the other hand, if

I say that some of the prophecy is *not* 'from the Lord', I shall be written off by the opposite wing who accuse me of 'being against the Spirit'!

If we can look hard at the 'Diana Prophecy' without adopting extreme positions, we may well discover that God is speaking to us and urging us to evangelize at a time of unprecedented opportunity. Our responsibility is not to quibble about prophecies but to be faithful to the Great Commission, otherwise we shall be guilty of 'fiddling while Rome burns'.

Are all parts of the prophecy equally authentic?

In my view, no. My reasons are stated (I trust clearly) under the previous question.

Is the prophecy glorifying Jesus Christ?

This is the most important test of all. I would say that the prophecy does glorify Jesus Christ. True, Part One did not mention Jesus at all, but the prophecy was not considered to be complete until Part Two was added to it on 31 August. Part Two speaks of the people knowing 'the joy of their salvation in the mighty risen Lord Jesus'.

Jesus is here declared as the way of salvation. He is declared as the mighty One, the Lord, and the One who has been raised from the dead. I call that glorifying Jesus! Ginny Burgin is not in the spotlight herself, and Princess Diana is not even mentioned by name, so the only person being glorified in the Diana Prophecy is the Lord Jesus.

Is the prophecy cutting across what has been taught from the Bible by introducing a completely new idea?

Clearly not. The prophecy is not directed only to the local church – namely, Walkley Baptist Church but is addressed to all Christians in Britain.

It might be objected that the emphasis on imminent revival is contrary to the New Testament's teaching, which lays the emphasis upon tribulation in the Last Days and our being prepared for it through faith and holiness. But it is precisely at this point that we need to acknowledge its imperfections and leave them aside. In fairness, a good deal of the clamour for revival has not come from the prophecy at all but rather from those picking it up and 'running with it', interpreting it in ways which suit their hopes and aspirations.

In summary

The 'Diana Prophecy' is amazing, but flawed. That is what we should expect, because even the greatest prophecies from God come through flawed individuals who unwittingly taint the pure word with their own 'contributions'. Paul himself said, 'Our prophecy is imperfect' (1 Corinthians 13:9).

But that does not make it invalid! It means we must exercise our faculties of discernment to tell truth from error. When we have done this to our own satisfaction and have a confirming witness of the Spirit, we need to respond to it.

What is the burden of the prophecy? Surely it is its powerful call to evangelism. If God has sent a message with the flowers and in the prophecy, it is a message of love. God loves His world and He longs to save. Jesus Christ, the divine Son, has come to the world to bring salvation through His death on the cross. He is raised from the dead and He is Lord.

The word of the Lord to His Church is what it ever was: 'All authority in heaven and on earth has been given to Me. Therefore go and make disciples of all nations (including your own), baptizing them into the Name of the Father and of the Son and of the Holy Spirit, and teaching them to obey everything I have commanded you. And surely I am with you always, to the very end of the age' (Matthew 28:18–20).

The Lord has said it – we are to *do* it.

'Revival is coming!'

Gerald Coates (and many other leaders of the Charismatic Movement) welcomed the whole 'prophecy', and considered it the harbinger of revival. Indeed, Gerald and other leaders associated with him were enthusiastically expecting signs of revival to be evident within two months of Diana's death.

Part One of the 'prophecy' states, '... I am on the move in the cities of this nation and where flowers are laid my Spirit will be moving faster than those flowers are removed.'

On 11 September, national news forecasters said it would take six weeks for workmen to clear the flowers. On this basis, Gerald reckoned the six week period in the 'prophecy' meant the period between 11 September and

23 October. He and others encouraged their followers to 'lay aside our personal priorities and even some of our local church activities and gather in Westminster [at the Emmanuel Evangelical Church Centre, Marsham Street] to pray for revival and get right with God.'

Much as one would like to say otherwise, there is no significant evidence to show, even months after the flowers were cleared, that the nation has experienced anything approaching revival, if historical descriptions are anything to go by. The need for God to revive the Church is pressing, but unless the longed-for revival is totally different from previous 'visitations', we can only conclude that it has not happened. Duncan Campbell, an eye-witness of the Hebridean Revival which broke out in 1949, described its effect upon the local communities. He said they were 'communities saturated with the presence of God!'

Looking at the well documented history of revivals, that would seem to be a fair and consistent description. Sadly we have not seen anything remotely like this during the weeks and months since the death of Diana, Princess of Wales. Much as we need it, we have yet to see signs of genuine revival in today's Britain. Claims are made that lively Christian meetings accompanied by strange manifestations are signs of genuine revival, but one fears they only echo the story of the Emperor's New Clothes. We are in danger of allowing our longing for true revival to lead us into inventing it, or at best to label things which are not marks of revival as if they were.

If history offers any encouragement, it is worth noting what happened in the eighteenth century. The upheavals of the late eighteenth century, especially the revolutions in America and France, were followed by a rapid decline in

Christian witness. Kenneth Scott Latourette in his *History of the Expansion of Christianity* (Eyre and Spottiswoode, 1937–45, 7 volumes) comments, 'it seemed as though Christianity were a waning influence, about to be ushered out of the affairs of men'.

The eighteenth century churches were in a desperate state and appeared to have little to say nor influence to bear in restraining the moral slide in individuals and whole communities. In desperation, pockets of concerned Christian leaders began to pray to God for His divine intervention. Six great waves of renewal of biblical Christianity and evangelism rocked America and Europe, and through phenomenal missionary endeavour changed the face of the globe.

Since the two world wars, the Church has again slipped away from its moorings in the Word of God, and is again considered 'a waning influence, about to be ushered out of the affairs of men'.

As then, so now. We need a revival. But what do we mean by that?

A synonym used consistently through the Church's history to describe revival is 'awakening'. Both 'revival' and 'awakening' refer to a return from a state of sleep to a state of consciousness. They do not denote what are often referred to these days as 'paradigm shifts', dramatic leaps into the new and untried, but rather a return to the state we were in before we went to sleep. Naturally enough, if the sleep has been deep the change of state to full consciousness is going to be quite a shock! But the important conclusion is that 'revival' is a return to *normality*, rather than a shift to an abnormal state. So we look for a return to the normal rather than a grasping for the spectacular and abnormal.

The normal life of the Church is clearly laid out in the New Testament: so a revived Church is a group of Christians living according to New Testament principles. A revived Christian is someone who is believing and living according to New Testament principles. The normal Christian life *is* New Testament life. Precisely that. No so-called revival can possibly exceed New Testament life and faith, because you cannot improve on the Bible!

The word 'revive' appears some eleven times in the Old Testament books, and twice in the New. According to Georg Fohrer's *Hebrew & Aramaic Dictionary of the Old Testament* (SCM Press, 1973) the Hebrew word *chayah* means 'live, remain alive, revive, recover'. So the meaning is clearly that of being restored to a former state of life, and not a new level in advance of the original state.

According to Arndt and Gingrich, (*op. cit.*, p 53) the New Testament Greek word *anazao* means 'come to life again or spring into life'. Again, the word means to restore to a former state of life and carries no thought of introducing a new level in advance of the original state.

This is far more than mere debate about words. It has very far-reaching consequences regarding the Church's focal point and hopes for the future.

5
Interesting Times

Confusion reigns supreme

There can be no question that people are gripped by a fascination for the paranormal. A recent *Daily Mail* poll revealed that there are as many people in Britain who believe in the paranormal as believe in God. (But although they boast fairness, the same amount of editorial space is not granted to God's spokesmen as is granted to the pundits of the paranormal!) Newspapers are stuffed with the paranormal and it is scarcely possible to sell a periodical unless it has a horoscope somewhere in its pages. Mystic Meg is unleashed on the National Lottery punters and psychic practitioners are consulted by a number of British police forces to assist in solving difficult cases.

Fun fairs and boot fairs now have to compete with psychic fairs and most shopping centres accommodate at least one New Age shop. *The X Files* commands enormous audiences and video games are becoming increasingly occult centred. It truly seems as if the paranormal is becoming normal. Big business indeed!

At the same time as fascination for the paranormal has grown, the invasion of new religions has advanced at a furious rate. Large-scale immigration coupled with 'political correctness' has created a situation where anything goes and goes rather well. The weakening of the Christian Church from outside pressures and from its own puzzling tendency to self-destruct has produced a generation of religious experimenters. Most fair-minded people perceive this as being 'a good thing' because it encourages a sense of unity within plurality: each man doing what seems good to him. A sense of 'live and let live' must surely be the civilized approach to life. So it is thought.

These days nobody can accuse the British of being atheistic. Religion is alive and well. We have more religions to choose from than at any time in our history! Christianity, Islam, Judaism, Hinduism, New Age paganism, Buddhism ... the list grows ever longer.

Our schoolchildren are no longer provided with a basic understanding of the Bible and the fundamentals of Christian faith. It is not unusual to find children who do not know who Jesus Christ is, let alone Moses or John the Baptist!

We may add to this the general air of confusion which predominates in much of the Church in Britain. Senior Church leaders have permitted some of their number to peddle doctrines which are simply contrary to Christian belief and life-styles which are both offensive to nature and alien to the Bible. It is small wonder that people have lost their confidence in the Church. Having lost their religious bearings they are fair game for anything, be it true or false.

Where have all the pillars gone?

Every society stands on a series of pillars. They are there to support it and form its foundation. They include the monarchy, Parliament, law and order, education, industry, food production, social services, the City, the armed forces, family life, public morality and, of course, the Church.

As we view history we can see that if any one of these pillars is weak or crumbling, those which remain intact can carry the extra weight. So despite the problems, society stands. But if a situation arises when several pillars become weak and crumbling at the same time, the position is much more serious. If *all* the pillars of society become weak and start crumbling at the same time, it is difficult to see how it can be saved.

At the risk of appearing to be prophets of doom and gloom, we have to face the fact that the erosion of our British way of life is well advanced. One does not need to be a genius to see that all the pillars of British society appear to be crumbling at once.

A crumbling monarchy?

After the collapse of royal marriages and the loss of respect for even the most senior members of the Royal Family, it is sad to reflect upon former days when the Royal Family represented the 'best of British'. The furore which greeted Her Majesty the Queen's apparent reluctance to lead the nation's mourning over Diana created hurt and resentment in the Royal Family. But it was thoroughly deserved.

The Royals completely misjudged the mood of the people not only with regard to Diana's loss but also to their own already tarnished public standing.

With the public memory of Princess Diana beginning to fade, Prince Charles appears to be regaining popularity to some degree. Tabloid newspapers carry photographs of him holding the hand of a little child with AIDS. Are his advisers trying to create a new image? Perhaps they have in mind establishing a new *King* of Hearts! To have to resort to such measures it looks as if the monarchy is fighting for its life. But in whatever state it survives, the monarchy can never be the same again.

Even the Church of England has adjusted its prayer responsibility for the Royal Family by altering the status of the state prayers in the modern Prayer Book (*The Alternative Service Book*, 1980). They are now a supplement which means they are sometimes included in Morning and Evening Prayer and sometimes not. We can only conclude that prayer for the Royal Family is no longer seen as a vital necessity within the daily worship of the Anglican Church: the Queen and her family are not considered as important within the life of the nation as they were. Just at the time when prayer to God on their behalf is most necessary, the Church of England decides to reduce its prayer commitment! Is it any wonder that the monarchy is crumbling?

One of the remaining symbols of the monarch's prestige was the royal yacht, *Britannia*. On 11 December 1997 she hosted the Queen's final reception on board for several thousand people who had served on the vessel through the years. Amid tears and genuine sadness the Royal Standard came down for the last time and the fine old ship ceased its distinguished career. The tradition of

337 years, which had produced a succession of magnificent royal yachts, came to an end. This was somehow a comment upon the changed status of the monarchy.

On a more trivial (but revealing) note, it is fascinating to see the press referring regularly to the country's First Lady as being the Prime Minister's wife, Cherie Blair, not the Queen! Times have changed.

A crumbling Parliament?

'You can't trust politicians!' That has always been the majority view. But in recent years the revelations of sleaze and the procession of U-turns and broken election promises have combined to undermine respect for ministers of the Crown and Members of Parliament in general. Staunch Labour supporters have been dumbfounded at some of the antics and anti-social policies now espoused by the government, policies which amount to a complete denial of election promises and of the very conscience of the Labour movement.

The 'image makers' and 'spin-doctors' have been busily engaged in re-educating the public's perception of both major parties. As regards the Labour government, we are encouraged to see them as great champions of the oppressed (though at times they appear to be screwing the oppressed into the ground!). Labour leaders tell us they wish to be known by their Christian names, and the familiar red face of the Left has lost all its wrinkles and floridity, being thoroughly rejuvenated, very friendly and terribly nice! The cosmetics are costly, but do they work? Many of us do not think so!

Those applying their cosmetic art to the Conservatives in opposition have striven to create a less remote and more 'matey' *persona grata*. The sight of Her Majesty's Opposition members in pullovers, trying to be hearty with each other as they engaged in a so-called 'bonding session' at their recent party conference, did nothing to boost confidence in a credible alternative government. It was as pathetic as it was funny.

But behind our shock and amazement lies a deeper fear. While on the surface at least so-called 'New Labour' seem to have a number of fresh ideas for government, there is an appalling suspicion that our politicians (whether male or female) are not man enough for the job. It feels to many of us as if the British Bulldog is hurtling towards a cliff edge and there is no handler with the wit or wisdom to check him. Times have changed!

Crumbling law and order?

Britain has changed dramatically in the last twenty years. Crime figures continue to alarm and in many towns and cities people are afraid to walk in the streets after dark. We have become a more violent people. New terms like 'road rage' are added to the list of crimes and even young children are guilty of murder. Mothers are caught on video camera as they brutalize their infants in hospital, and parental abuse – particularly by fathers – has become a monotonous testimony in doctors' and counsellors' surgeries. Terrorism has spread its web of fear over the whole of society. Precautionary measures cause disruption and cost the country untold millions.

Time was when our judicial system was the envy of the world. Getting a fair trial with a fair sentence could be expected in the vast majority of cases. Public anxiety over miscarriages of justice is now mounting. Ridiculously lenient sentences handed out to hardened criminals undermine our confidence in the rule of law and leave society feeling unprotected. When people lose confidence in the appointed watchmen over the nation's behaviour, they tend to take the law into their own hands out of sheer frustration. Anarchy then rears its head.

The recent revelations of Sir Paul Condon, laying bare his personal worry over the high percentage of 'bent officers' within the Metropolitan Police, produced a shudder of disbelief. A number of forces throughout the country have been exposed as having police officers found guilty of gross misconduct. When we are unable to trust our police officers, and discover that many are themselves practising criminals, things have become desperate. Our system of law and order appears to be crumbling.

A crumbling education system?

Morale among teachers in British schools has never been lower. Teachers are subjected to pupil abuse and yet are deprived of the means to discipline. Performance tables and financial restrictions feed frustration and many teachers feel that the nation no longer values their work. Truth to tell, the standard of teaching in some schools leaves a great deal to be desired, and with a multitude of children leaving school with little or no reading skills, or facility with figures, something is obviously amiss.

We are told that an underclass has emerged made up of uneducated and disaffected young people for whom the prospect of work is as unwelcome as it is unlikely.

Morale among students at colleges of higher education is also low. Many colleges are seedbeds of immorality and paganism and for those students who succeed in obtaining their degree career prospects are far from certain. To the anxious observer the entire education system appears to be crumbling.

A crumbling industry?

Shipbuilding, coal mining, steel production ... virtually all gone. All gone where? All gone to other parts of the world. We are now forced to import what we used to export, and multitudes in our national workforce pour through the doors of social security offices where once they crowded through the factory gates.

It is encouraging to see the great strides made in the high technology, commercial and service industries, but to lose our capabilities in producing basic materials is dangerous. Heavy industry has become lightweight. Our industrial base has lost most of its foundations and we are dependent for our raw materials on the good offices of other nations. It is depressing indeed to see our proud reputation as a major industrial power in the world crumbling right away, and our vulnerability to the vagaries of international relations is alarming.

Crumbling agriculture and fisheries?

Almost every week brings fresh news of disaster for farmers and fishermen. The decimation of beef farming has been a national disgrace of historic proportions. The BSE scare has cost us dear and lamb seems at risk of following the sad demise of beef. It is tragic to see years of investment and devotion to the creating of pedigree herds and flocks simply being cast aside.

The curious thing is that those industrialists who unscrupulously promoted the use of animal offal in feeding herbivores appear to go completely unpunished, while the victim of the situation – the British farmer – is punished. Strange indeed. Why is no one brought to book?

The agricultural policies of the Council of Europe seem to have been aimed at destroying British farming at all levels. There is a new war in Europe – an economic one – and Britain is decidedly on the losing side. Our fishermen have had their industry carved up almost to the point of extinction, and to visit most of our traditional fishing harbours is a sad experience. Tradition remains: fishing is gone.

From being a nation well able to feed itself we have degenerated to the point of being substantially dependent upon imports from other countries in Europe and much from elsewhere. This trend is very much in accord with the aspirations of New Age pundits who espouse so-called New World Order policies to force states to become interdependent. The history of Europe as we have seen it, with its capacity for violent and sudden change, means that we find ourselves in a precarious position. Our farming heritage is crumbling.

Crumbling health and social services?

Lengthening queues for surgery, the closure of hospitals, impossible pressures upon hospital medical staff and GPs, combine to show that the once noble National Health Service now is scarcely visible.

Who among us is not alarmed at the falling standards, limited resources and low staff morale? Patient care is placed way below financial viability in the order of priorities. Apart from those wealthy enough to pay for private treatment, our people dread the prospect of old age and the possibility of sickness.

The mentally sick in the community and those who support them have suffered a terrible blow in the previous government's 'Care in the Community' policy. Many people, quite unable to look after themselves – some a proven danger to society – have been released and their hospitals closed. Many needing support to cope have found the social services woefully inadequate, and for many needing positive care it has been non-existent. There have been appalling consequences of this policy, with great distress for patients, relatives and neighbours. One former patient suggested on BBC Radio 4 that 'Care in the Community' should more correctly be called 'Neglect in the Community'.

No one would suggest that the solution is going to be easy. Hospitals for the mentally sick that have been closed cannot easily be reopened and there is a very serious shortage of doctors coming into the mental health sector due to low morale and lack of funding. Health care costs vast sums and it is difficult to see how any government can make the hard choices in terms of massive increases in taxation which could reverse the decline. Self preservation is a very powerful motive where governments are concerned.

Our culture has produced a generation replete with single-parent families, an ever increasing population of the elderly, AIDS sufferers, drug dependants. This costs money – vast amounts of money. Where can it be found? Governments shunt revenue from one place to another, but if they attempt to raise new money by increased taxation they find it is political suicide and so the problem gets worse by the day.

In spite of the government's best efforts to reduce the number of unemployed and unemployable, the numbers create vast need of financial support. Among the genuine and deserving there are also those in our society who have made a career in studying ways to 'screw' the nation for every farthing they can in social benefits. This is costing us dear. Many have a sense that things are getting out of control. Another crumbling pillar?

The crumbling City?

The Lloyds crash of 1994 sent shock waves across the world. Who would have thought it? One of Britain's cast-iron institutions brought to the very brink of collapse, and all apparently because of greed. City institutions have been shown to be vulnerable, not only to the vagaries of foreign markets but also to unscrupulous traders within.

Many commentators are predicting what amounts to an 'earthquake' in the City, which will have catastrophic consequences for the financial heart of the nation.

Crumbling armed forces?

The deliberate running down of our defence capability has taken place on an escalating scale ever since the Second World War. Now, according to senior military opinion, the situation is beyond reason. Britain's ability to defend itself depends on alliances with foreign powers. This is all very well when relationships are good, but history shows that there is little wisdom in making ourselves too dependent upon our European or even transatlantic neighbours!

Our military capability as a sovereign nation has suffered such decimation in every branch of the services that without help there is no way we can defend ourselves against an aggressor. Our military defences have crumbled.

A crumbling Church

In the River Thames, just across from the Tower of London, lies an enormous battle cruiser, HMS *Belfast*, the largest cruiser ever built for the Royal Navy. Every year thousands of visitors pour over her, admiring her lines, marvelling at her history and gawping at her armaments.

It's a long time since the *Belfast* fired a shot in anger. Her powerful guns are disarmed and silent and those who admire her do so only on account of what was, not for what is.

All over the country, in town and village, once-proud church buildings now stand empty and silent. Anglican churches and Nonconformist chapels have been turned into houses, craft centres, arts centres and restaurants.

Some have been sold off as mosques or temples or carpet warehouses. One thing is certain, they are not required for the purpose their builders had in mind: the worship of Jesus Christ and the preaching of the gospel.

The vast numbers of casualties on the battlefields of the First World War denuded the Church in Britain of its men. The Second World War, twenty years later, compounded the problem. Mothers went to church alone with their children or simply sent them along to Sunday school. When the fathers returned from the war they did not return to their places of worship. So the Church in Britain suffered disastrous body blows with the loss of so many of its men. As a consequence the impression was formed that churchgoing was for womenfolk, the elderly and children, not for red-blooded men.

To be frank, many churches had little to offer. Liberalism had neutered the gospel and removed its vigour. The Bible was despised and so revelation of Jesus Christ became warped and paganized. A lot of the so-called 'preaching' amounted to little more than humanism with a religious veneer. The idea became popular that Christianity needed to be stripped of its religious 'mumbo jumbo', sin, miracles and 'all that stuff' and the universal brotherhood of man proclaimed loud and clear. The passage of time has shown that the wholesale move towards a kind of populist religion has failed dismally.

In today's Britain, the Church is seen to be largely irrelevant. The clergy are largely to blame for this because they have abandoned the faith of the Bible. As this has happened the Church has been stripped of its *true* power – the power of God's Holy Spirit – and is left with 'ecclesiastical power', which is little better than an empty nest after the dove has flown. When ordinary people are asked what members of society they turn to in time of need, the clergy come way down the scale. Ahead of them are doctors, solicitors, psychiatrists, New Age practitioners, TV personalities – even the neighbour's cat!

While it is certainly true that there is an increasing number of truly Bible-believing Christians in this country, they are still a tiny minority. The vast edifice of the traditional Church is crumbling away fast.

6

'Who is Speaking?'

'Is there anyone out there?'

One of the fascinating areas of modern conjecture concerns interstellar communication. Are there intelligences beyond our own which can communicate with us?

Many would like to think so. The idea that out of all the planets in all of the universes, the earth alone is home to the sole possessors of intelligence, is simply unreasonable to them. There simply *must* be other beings somewhere with communication skills to match or exceed our own! But are there? Could it be that in the purposes of God this tiny planet, Earth, is utterly unique and that it is the sole place of life amidst all the galaxies of all the universes?

Around the world there are scientists who devote their time to attempting to find signals coming from distant galaxies. *Anything* to show we are not alone! Many wonder if UFOs offer some encouragement. A magnetic attraction combined with deep-seated fear draws our interest. We want to know, and yet we do not want to know.

Making the connection

We all share some measure of longing for companionship. It appears to be inborn. Companionship is basic to living in every culture. Indeed, the survival of all life is dependent upon it! It is such a strong driving force. But where does it come from? According to Genesis 2:18, the Lord God said, 'It is not good for man to be alone. I will make a helper suitable for him.'

God had just created the earth and everything in it. Adam was his supreme creation, made in His image. But companionship was essential for Adam's well-being. God brought all the animals and birds to Adam. They were wonderful. Some of them would make delightful companions ... but there was something missing. An indefinable yearning which the animals could not satisfy. Genesis 2:20 says:

> But for Adam no suitable helper was found. So the Lord God caused Adam to fall into a deep sleep; and while he was sleeping, He took one of Adam's ribs and closed up the place with flesh. Then the Lord God made a woman from the rib He had taken out of Adam, and He brought her to him.
>
> Adam said, 'This is now bone of my bones and flesh of my flesh; she shall be called 'woman', for she was taken out of man.'
>
> For this reason a man will leave his father and mother and be united to his wife, and they will become one flesh.

The Lord God provided Adam with someone who satisfied his longing for companionship – Eve. The union was ideal. Adam and Eve – together they were one flesh, companions indeed in the perfection of Eden.

But the essential factor is that this was not a two-partner companionship. There was a third party – God Himself. With God in the relationship Adam and Eve knew the true bliss of companionship, where no longing for 'something more' remained in their hearts.

'Adam, where are you?'

Disaster struck the garden, a blight so terrible that all creation was poisoned. Adam and Eve turned against God. Rebellion entered the idyll of Eden. The consequence was appalling – a dislocation from God.

Everything changed in an instant. Companionship with God was at an end and even the level of relationship between Adam and Eve was changed. With God in the relationship there was bliss. Without God in the relationship something indefinable but profound had been lost. Humanly speaking it could never be the same again.

One of the most poignant moments in all recorded history comes at this point, described in Genesis 3:8:

> Then Adam and his wife heard the sound of the Lord God as He was walking in the garden in the cool of the day, and they hid from the Lord God among the trees of the garden. But the Lord God called to Adam, 'Where are you?'

He answered, 'I heard you in the garden, and I was
afraid because I was naked; so I hid.'

The Fall of Adam and Eve was not only a disaster for man,
it was also a disaster for God. The companionship was at
an end. The impression given by Moses (who wrote up the
account) is that it was God's custom to come to the garden
regularly. He came simply to enjoy the companionship of
Adam and Eve. It was entirely reciprocal: they all shared
the joy ... all the time. That is simply the delightful way
things were – until the Fall.

The faithfulness of God

Companionship with God and all this brought to the
well-being of Adam and Eve was thus lost. Something
died in them. Something was lost also to the Lord God.
He had created Adam and Eve for His own sake as well as
for theirs. So in the Fall God was deprived as well as man.

The estrangement of the ages began. From that point
onwards God's longing for the companionship of man
was frustrated, thwarted by man's rebellion. Even so He
made faithful provision for man's material needs and also
continued to speak to men and women who showed an
inclination to know Him and love Him. This revelation of
His word found particular expression in the provision of
what we call the Hebrew Scriptures – documents written
by God-fearing men which record God's words and
actions in the history of the Hebrew people.

In these various documents law, history, prophecy and
poetry combined to reveal God's heart and will to those

who felt their need of companionship with Him. For there were people who, sensing a terrible void in their lives, longed to 'come home' to God and enjoy His fellowship. There had been such people from the earliest days after the Fall – people like Noah and his family. They were followed by a great procession of faithful Hebrews – Abraham and Sarah, Jacob and Rachel, Isaac and Rebekah, Moses, Joshua, David, Elijah, Isaiah, Daniel ... men and women who had *faith*. Implicit trust in God, often within violently hostile cultures and situations.

How had they managed to find God, given that sin had created an impenetrable barrier? The answer lies in the heart of God. Estranged or otherwise, He still longed for man's companionship and so He chose to *reveal* Himself to those He knew would respond, given the opportunity. First to individuals like Noah, Abraham and Isaac, then to the family of Jacob, which in the course of time became the nation of Israel.

God's dilemma

There was an underlying factor which made it possible for God the Father to reach out to man. In His perfect knowledge He planned a way for His relationship with man to be restored. Sin had created an impenetrable barrier and could not be ignored. Punishment was due if God's innate sense of justice was to be upheld. But at the same time God's burning love for man made it impossible for the due punishment to be delivered. The judicial punishment of sin would mean nothing short of death for all mankind. How would God resolve the dilemma? How could love and justice meet?

The answer was as unthinkable as it was brilliant. God must take the punishment Himself as man's substitute. This would satisfy God's love and His justice too.

From all eternity God's person was so vastly huge and unimaginable that His personhood was expressed as three Persons in One – Father, Son and Holy Spirit. These three titles are the closest which finite language can come to expressing the infinite truth about God. They are wonderful words carrying wonderful concepts, although no human words can bring us to the final truth about the infinite, holy God. But they come as close as we can get.

This is the reason we find it difficult to understand how in allowing Jesus Christ to be our substitute as He suffered death for us, God was actually punishing *Himself*. The fact remains, that is exactly what happened. John 3:16 puts it this way: 'For God so loved the world that He gave His only begotten Son, that whoever believes in Him shall not perish but have eternal life.'

So the remarkable fact is that it was the death of Jesus Christ which made it possible for man once more to find companionship with God. And this was the focus of faith for the people of the Hebrew Scriptures – the Old Testament – as well as for those who have believed since Christ died.

Man's dilemma

From the moment Adam fell, man was constantly aware of a need for the companionship of God. Companionship with wife, family and friends was not enough. There was a void in the life of man which needed to be filled in some way. So began the quest for a personality or force beyond the created order to which man could relate.

Here lies the origin of religion. Religion is man's attempt to find relationship with a god other than the true God. The fact that he believes he has found such 'gods' convinces him that they are legitimate substitutes. But in truth this is a delusion. The words of Jesus Christ in John 14:6 are unequivocal: 'I am *the* way, *the* truth and *the* life. No one comes to the Father except through me.'

Man has always considered that there are many ways to find God. Some have likened it to climbing a mountain by various routes, some better defined than others. Each is different, but all reach the same summit. This may be an appealing idea, but according to Jesus Christ it is wrong. Quite clearly, *He* is the only One who can lead us to the Father: He alone.

The message

So in answer to the question, 'Has God spoken?' we may leave the definitive answer with the person who wrote the Letter to the Hebrews (see Hebrews 1:1): 'In the past God spoke to our forefathers through the prophets at many times and in various ways, but in these last days He has spoken to us by His Son ...'

God *has* spoken. And the News is very good!

7

The Scandal of the Cross

It is a terrible scandal to see the way in which biblical Christianity has been maligned and misrepresented through the centuries. But much of that is thoroughly deserved. Things done in the name of Christ have often displayed a complete ignorance or disregard of the gospel and have expressed more of the devil than of the Saviour.

The first visit I ever paid to Israel taught me a big history lesson. My family and I were enjoying a relaxing day on the beach at Netanya. To my great satisfaction I had succeeded in building a rather splendid sand-castle. There it stood, complete with moat and bridge, its keep and turrets standing proud. Like all self-respecting castles it had loopholes all over it, and I reproduced them as typical Norman loopholes, shaped like elongated crosses. Though I say it myself, it was a good castle. The children were impressed. Mission accomplished!

I lay back in the sun and snoozed. Suddenly I was woken by shouts and sat up to see a Jewish man in his fifties jumping all over my sand-castle and making every effort to destroy it! I sprang to my feet at this international incident and expressed my indignation in no uncertain terms. He in turn rounded on me and spat out a statement which lives with me still:

'You have made a Crusader castle. We HATE the cross in Israel. How dare you build such a hateful thing here!'

To say I was shocked would be to understate. I was speechless. The man strode purposefully away across the sand and I was left to ponder what I had heard. 'We hate the cross in Israel ... ' But why?

In answering that question we reach into history and find some compelling reasons. Not only to explain the hatred of the Jews, but also to explain the incredulity and contempt of millions for the Church and everything associated with it.

Constantine the Great

It was an October day in the year 312 AD. Two great armies of Roman troops converged on a point just to the north of Rome. Each was led by a claimant to the imperial throne, Maxentius and Constantine.

Constantine had been proclaimed emperor six years before on the death of his father by his loyal troops at York, but this proclamation was not ratified officially because three other claimants emerged. Constantine now marched to confront one of them in the decisive battle at the Milvian Bridge.

According to his biographer, Eusebius, Constantine had a vision before the engagement. He saw a cross emblazoned across the sky together with an inscription, *In hoc signe vinces*, 'In this sign you will conquer'. Constantine won the battle at the Milvian Bridge and it was to prove a turning point in history.

The victorious Constantine immediately assumed the vision to be a divine sign from heaven indicating that Christianity must be made the official religion of his empire and that this would guarantee his position as absolute ruler. He took the first two letters of Christ's name (the Greek *chi* and *rho*) and superimposing one letter upon the other, made it his official emblem. He emerged as sole emperor after his victory in the battle at Chrysopolis in 324 and from that time was known as the first Christian emperor.

Ever since the days of the apostles, Christianity had been an illegal religion in the Roman Empire. Called *religio illicita*, it was not tolerated and those who practised it were branded as criminals and suffered the consequences. The emperor Nero had initiated capital punishment for Christians following the disastrous fire in Rome in the summer of 64 AD. He held them responsible, though they were probably totally innocent, and their already extreme public unpopularity made them easy scapegoats. Contemporary writers like Tacitus describe the most barbaric treatment of Christians in Rome. He writes,

> Besides being put to death, [Christians] were made to serve as objects of amusement: they were clad in the hides of animals and torn to death by dogs; others were crucified, others set on fire to serve to illuminate the night when daylight failed. Nero had thrown open his grounds for the display, and was putting on a show in the circus, where he mingled with the people in the dress of a charioteer or drove about in his

> chariot. All this gave rise to a feeling of pity ... for it
> was felt that they were being destroyed not for the
> public good but to gratify the cruelty of an individual.
> (Annals, xv.44)

In spite of continuing persecution through the following three centuries Christian congregations had held their ground numerically and there were believers among a number of influential Roman families. But the 'conversion' of Constantine brought about a wedding between Church and state, and even meant a diverting of imperial funds into the strong-boxes of the Church. Bishops took on affairs of state as well as ecclesiastical duties and in its turn imperial regulation invaded the Church. By any standards, this was a disaster for the Church. It represented a fusion of Christianity with paganism, the legacy of which has bedevilled Christian faith and witness ever since.

It had begun with the famous 'vision' in the sky which Constantine interpreted as being a good omen from heaven. But it may properly be asked if his assumption was correct. Was it really from God? If so, which one? Constantine's family worshipped Apollo, the Unconquered Sun, and it is unquestionable that certain features of sun worship were incorporated into the 'new' Roman Church. Among these were the adoption of sunrise services and the 'sunburst' as a central motif on the communion table, which now became an altar. Many features and symbols from the Mystery religions were blended with Christian revelation to create an empire-wide Roman Church which was to dominate vast areas of the world until the time of the Protestant Reformation twelve centuries later.

Was Jesus Christ represented by the 'cross' which Constantine supposedly saw? It is at best questionable. For one thing, how could the authentic voice of Jesus Christ, the Prince of Peace, encourage a Roman general to butcher legions of enemy troops? This is what we are asked to believe if the 'voice' saying, 'By this sign, conquer!' was the authentic voice of God.

Nor was it only enemy Roman troops who were treated to Constantine's 'Christian' brutality. For the Jews, the era of persecution by pagan Romans was passing away only to be replaced by even worse and prolonged persecutions by 'Christian' Romans. Constantine elevated the clergy to heights of power which enabled them to enter upon a terrible and cruel campaign against the Jews. Massacres of Jews were commonplace, and the burning of synagogues became a 'Christian' sport. In all these activities the 'cross' was the prominent symbol, and it immediately became synonymous with anti-Semitism.

When knights were bold ...

As a child I always admired the crusaders. To me they represented everything that was noble and good. King Richard the 'Lion Heart' was one of my heroes, and my fertile imagination easily conjured up the shimmering sight of the armoured knights riding to meet the Moslem armies of Saladin. I viewed it all as a high point in our nation's history. The crusaders marching to free the Holy Land from the tyranny of Islam – their hauberks, shields and banners emblazoned with the red cross of Christ. This was the stuff of adventure and courage, of chivalry and right. Made in England!

Nor was this a private view. History books and childhood stories painted a similar picture. The story of Robin Hood and his Merry Men, to name but one, fed the notion that good King Richard was away fighting in a most noble cause and would one day return to oust the dastardly Prince John and re-establish his own righteous reign.

Then I woke up. The truth is that the Crusades (from the Latin *crux*, meaning cross) were a terrible blight upon the name of Christ and the witness of the Church.

In 1071 Turkish Moslem forces had won a decisive battle at Manzikert and the eastern emperor of Constantinople appealed to Pope Urban II to come to his aid. In 1095 the Pope put out a powerful appeal across Europe, stressing the need to take the Holy City, Jerusalem, from the Moslems. Thousands responded to this appeal and a huge mob of 50,000 poured through Europe to Constantinople and across the Bosporus into Asia Minor. The First Crusade eventually reached Jerusalem and took it from the Moslems in 1099. Over the next 200 years a succession of so-called crusaders came into Israel, some nobility but most of them adventurers motivated by bloodlust and hopes of plunder rather than principle.

The crusaders were driven by fanatical ideas which filled them with hatred not only for Moslems but also for Jews. They slaughtered, tortured, raped and pillaged thousands of Jews in the belief that *as a race* they were responsible for the death of Jesus.

Admittedly there were some Christian voices raised in protest during the period, notably St Bernard of Clairvaux, but to little effect. The crusaders rampaged through Asia

Minor and Israel leaving carnage in their wake. The red cross which adorned them became the symbol of death and misery to every Moslem and Jew.

Scandals associated with the cross of Jesus continued throughout the Middle Ages and beyond. The Spanish Inquisition targeted Jews and many were executed in ghastly circumstances with the cross held high by their tormentors. With the dawning of the modern era, it might be imagined that we would see the passing of the barbaric misuse of Christianity as an excuse for genocide and violence – but not a bit of it.

The Third Reich

The rise of Hitler and the National Socialists resulting in the Second World War besmirched the cross of Jesus with evil. 'The Holocaust was the work of Christians ... and the fulfilment of Christianity.' This was the considered opinion of the Israeli defence attorney in the trial of John Demjanjuk, accused of being 'Ivan the Terrible' at the infamous Treblinka death camp.

It is a conclusion which shocks and surprises, yet it is genuine. Why? In the first place Adolf Hitler claimed to be a Christian. He was born and reared a Catholic. He abandoned whatever Christian principles he possessed in favour of the secular philosophies of his day, but he never cut his ties with the Catholic Church, nor was he ever excommunicated. He cunningly used the Bible and Christianity to win over the support of German Christians. On 12 April 1922, he made a speech in which he said,

In boundless love, as a Christian and a human being,
I read the passage which tells us how the Lord at last
rose in his might and seized the scourge to drive out
of the Temple the brood of vipers and adders. How
terrific was His fight against the Jewish poison; I realize more profoundly than ever before the fact that
it was for this that He had to shed his blood upon
the Cross.

Such duplicitous thinking actually impressed many
German Christians and a motto frequently heard from
them was, 'The Swastika on our breasts, the Cross in our
hearts.'

The Nazi state and its pernicious effects upon the
churches, both Catholic and Protestant, caused powerful
internal struggles as Christians tried to come to terms
with what was taking place. Many true believers suffered
for their heroic stand against Hitler, but a vast number of
others acquiesced.

Pope Pius XI had praised Mussolini, the Italian dictator
as 'a man sent by Providence'. His successor, Pope Pius
XII, now chose to remain silent over the evils of Hitler's
Nazism. Thus the impression was given that Christianity
sanctioned war and wickedness.

'Christian' Hitler's loathing of the Jews is legendary. In
Mein Kampf he wrote, 'I hated the mixture of races
displayed in the capital [i.e. Vienna], I hated the motley
collection of Czechs, Poles, Hungarians, Ruthenians,
Croats, etc, and above all, that ever-present fungoid
growth – Jews, and again Jews.'

Hitler was supported in his frightful beliefs by statements made by the great Reformer, Martin Luther. In his

twilight years Luther's opinion of Jewish people went through a frightening change. In his early life he had been a supporter of Jews, as might be expected of an avid student of the Bible, but because of their resistance to conversion he later adopted what can only be described as a wickedly spiteful attitude which is amply reflected in his later writing. In a tract he wrote shortly before his death, Luther said,

The Jews deserve the most severe penalties. Their synagogues should be levelled, their homes destroyed, they should be exiled into tents like gypsies. Their religious writings should be taken from them. The rabbis should be forbidden to continue teaching the Law. All professions should be closed to them. Only the hardest, coarsest work should be permitted them. Rich Jews should have their fortunes confiscated, and the money used to support Jews who are willing to be converted. If all these measures are unsuccessful, the Christian princes have the duty of driving the Jews from their lands as they would rabid dogs.

In his book, *The Rise and Fall of the Third Reich* (Mandarin, 1991), W.L. Shirer wrote:

It is difficult to understand the behaviour of most German Protestants in the first Nazi years unless one is aware of two things: their history and the influence of Martin Luther. The great founder of Protestantism was both a passionate anti-Semite and a ferocious believer in absolute obedience to political authority.

He wanted Germany rid of the Jews ... advice that was literally followed four centuries later by Hitler, Goering and Himmler ... Luther employed a coarseness of language unequalled in German history until the Nazi time ... In no country, with the exception of Tsarist Russia, did the clergy become by tradition so completely servile to the political authority of the State.

It is small wonder the Jews find the cross offensive. Indeed, many view the 'swastika' as a representation of the cross. Truth to tell, it is more likely to be an occult symbol. However, leaving the swastika aside, we have only to look at photographs of Nazi officers, with their Iron Crosses adorning their throats, to see justification for the hideous association of ruthless cruelty with the faith we Christians profess. Closer to home, we see the same terrible association of the cross of Jesus and national hatred in the troubles in Northern Ireland.

'When Irish eyes are weeping ...'

The smothering of true Christian belief by political ambition was a tendency in the Church's history from the very start. It is no less true today. As we lurch from one crisis to another in the troubled borderlands between Eire and Northern Ireland, we see a deep-seated political divide cloaked in a religious garb. The labels 'Protestant' and 'Catholic' are used with great freedom to describe people who by their contentious, sectarian, even sometimes murderous attitudes, intentions and activities show themselves to be anything but Christian. That is, if we take the New Testament definition of Christian as authentic, which presumably we should.

We could mention the evils of the American slave trade, the deprivation and slaughter of American Indians, Victorian wars against African tribesmen ... all perpetrated with ruthlessness and association with the 'advance' of Christianity. We could point to the carnage in Rwanda as 'Christians' allow their primitive tribalism to drive them to unspeakable acts of torture.

Further cataloguing of the Church's failures in its witness is easy, but enough has been said. What has been written could be duplicated all over the world. In age after age, country by country, the cross of Christ has been made into a symbol of oppression and hatred.

Let the record stand. But let it stand as a dreadful warning. When biblical faith and the transforming power of Christ are replaced by political or ecclesiastical power all kinds of wicked possibilities loom large. History is strewn with scandalous examples, but we are left with the question, 'What now?'

Apologizing for the sins of our fathers?

It has always seemed to me extraordinary that a person should be asked to apologize on behalf of someone else, especially if that person is dead. Even the power of attorney cannot be given retrospectively, so how can confession and forgiveness be retrospective?

When people come on my Israel tours, we visit the Holocaust Museum in Jerusalem. There are usually members of the group, British or German, who wish to apologize to my Israeli guide for the atrocities committed against the Jewish people during the Nazi time. It is understandable that German Christians should be tormented by the experience, but it comes as a terrible shock for the British to see that we bear a heavy responsibility for doing so little to prevent the Holocaust and later for preventing refugees from entering Israel. A typical reaction by the members of my tour groups is to want to find our Jewish guide and ask for forgiveness.

My guides always respond with great grace, but gently point out that the members of the tour group were not responsible and in any event, how could they accept the apology and express forgiveness when they themselves were not even born at the time?

Apology and acceptance deal with a situation and lay it to rest. It is, as they say, 'done and dusted'. This should be a regular experience concerning our interpersonal relationships so that resentment is not allowed to build up. But it is a very *personal* matter. If, therefore, we ourselves have the same attitudes as our forebears, there is definite need for apology. But only for our attitudes: not for those of our forebears.

So what of those situations where we are identified with events through family ties or nationality? If personal apology is not appropriate, what is? Surely we need to express genuine regret that such things were done by our forebears or associates and declare our firm determination to ensure that *we* will not fall into the same pattern of belief and behaviour. This is a positive and practical answer to the problem and not a sentimental reaction to it.

How must God feel?

It is difficult to imagine the depth of sorrow God feels about the catalogue of dreadful things that have been done throughout history by those claiming to be Christian.

'If *that's* Christianity, you can keep it!' Who can blame people for adopting that kind of attitude when those who claim to be followers of Jesus act in a way which offends everything He represents? They are quite right to want to distance themselves from the Christian faith. Given the same set of circumstances, I expect Jesus would do the same! The attitudes and actions of the Nazis, crusaders, Irish terrorists and their ilk are a gross offence to the name of Christ.

But it has to be admitted that even without the more grotesque aberrations in the history of Christendom, there is much in the witness of the modern Church which offends people and forces them to conclude that Christians are merely a bunch of hypocrites.

The word 'hypocrite' is an anglicized form of the Greek word *hupokrisia*, which means 'actor'. To be a self-confessed follower of Christ but to live by totally different standards from His disgusts decent people and acts as an impenetrable barrier to faith. We may have every sympathy with the seeker who said to a preacher, 'I cannot hear what you say because what you *are* is shouting so loudly!'

It is high time we Christians put our house in order. There needs to be consistency between our profession and our practice. The Christian faith is more than a set of beliefs – it is a way of life. And this is no ordinary, respectable life – it is none other than the life of Jesus

Christ in us. When people begin to see that, their attitude will change. But if they cannot see it, who can blame them for being incredulous?

The blame for such incredulity must lie at the door of the Church. When Jesus said 'You are the light of the world' (Matthew 5:14), He added a defining comment: '... let your light shine before men, that they may see your good deeds and praise your Father in heaven.' So the light of the Church is the quality of its life – its good deeds. Jesus insists, 'You *are* the light of the world'. Jesus is not merely calling us to acts of philanthropy when He calls us to 'good deeds'. He means *godly living* at every level.

We Christians need to repent and to change, and to do it without further delay. If we do not turn away from iniquity and back to the Lord and the holy standards of the Bible, the prospect for us is inescapably one of judgement.

We may laugh it off and excuse ourselves all we like, but we Christians have placed ourselves in a very dangerous situation. God loves His world – Jesus Christ died for it. But so many of us who call ourselves followers of Christ have become obsessed with personal blessing and 'spiritual' experiences, even allowing thoroughly devilish ideas to invade our pulpits and strange unbiblical teachings to go unchallenged. We have turned a blind eye to the Lord's call to holiness and readiness for His return. We need to return to the Lord while there is still time.

Jesus likes sinners!

It is beyond question that vast numbers of people have rejected Christ because of the huge barrier formed by the Church. They look at the bloody history, they puzzle over the conflicting messages, they view with disdain the moral ineptitude, and conclude that Church is not for them.

Having said that, there is an innate longing for God in every created soul. When this is not met by a fulfilling relationship with Him through Christ, it is met by other things – false religion of one kind or another, ranging from Islam through to atheism. All belief systems (even a supposed lack of them) are substitutes for the Truth which can only be found in the God who reveals Himself in the Bible and in His Son, Jesus Christ, who said, 'I am the truth'.

So a deep longing for Father God is to be found in every man and woman, of whatever colour, age or disposition. How that longing is to be fulfilled is the great question.

When Jesus was here in person, He travelled the roads of Israel healing, releasing from demons, and revealing God's heart, mind and will through His preaching and His character. The 'ordinary' people loved Him and accepted Him. Those who hated and opposed Him tended to come from the traditional, religious community, particularly the priests, scribes and Pharisees.

We might have expected the opposite to be true. Surely those of a more religious disposition would be the ones to welcome Jesus, while the general public would reject Him. Why the strange role reversal? To understand this it is necessary to know something of the background world of the New Testament.

The Jews suffered a terrible blow when the southern part of Israel – that is, Judaea – was overrun by the Babylonians in 586 BC. King Nebuchadnezzar deported vast numbers and destroyed the great Temple of Solomon in Jerusalem. The national distress caused by this disaster is well expressed in Psalm 137:

> By the rivers of Babylon we sat down and wept when
>   we remembered Zion [Jerusalem].
> There on the poplars we hung our harps, for there our
>   captors asked us for songs of joy: they said
> 'Sing us one of the songs of Zion!'
> How can we sing the songs of the Lord while in a
>   foreign land?
> If I forget you, O Jerusalem, may my right hand forget
>   its skill. May my tongue cling to the roof of my
>   mouth if I do not remember you, if I do not con-
>   sider Jerusalem my highest joy.

The use of the past tense indicates that the writer was no longer in Babylon. In fact the captivity lasted until 538 BC, then the Persian conquerors of Babylon allowed the Jews to return to Judaea. So the psalm may well have been written then. During the years of captivity, marauding groups of Edomite Arabs from the south had vandalized what remained of Jerusalem and its Temple, and on returning to his capital the Jewish psalm writer saw the general devastation caused and commented,

> Remember, O Lord, what the Edomites did on the
>   day Jerusalem fell.
> 'Tear it down,' they cried, 'tear it down to its founda-
>   tions!'

When Nebuchadnezzar had invaded the Land and destroyed the Temple it looked as if the Jews might cease to exist as a nation. He ripped them away from their roots and it was no longer possible to express their faith in the God-ordained ways because that required sacrifice in the Temple. Without their Temple the Jews' national identity was severely threatened in their exile.

The threat was averted by the emergence of a new class of religious leader, the scribe. The focus of Jewish religion shifted from the Temple to the Law of Moses contained in the Torah, the first five books of the Hebrew Scriptures. Groups of Jews gathered together to hear the Law read and expounded. In this way, the Jews' sense of national identity was preserved. But the basis was no longer Temple sacrifice, it was adherence to the Law.

After the Persian liberation and their return to the Land, the Jews rebuilt the Temple and the sacrificial system started once more. However the synagogues – the gatherings for study of the Law – continued alongside Temple worship and became the regular, weekly focus of spiritual activity in Israel.

While there was only one Temple – in Jerusalem – there were synagogues in every town and village. Sometimes special buildings were constructed, sometimes homes were used. But the emphasis was always the same: exposition of the Law of Moses and practical help in obeying it to the letter. The Law had taken on a level of importance which sometimes bordered upon idolatry, as Jewish teachers spent their time analysing the minutiae of words and phrases and comparing the interpretations of noted rabbis with one another.

In order to guard the holy Law – the exact words of God in the Scripture text – the rabbis developed an ingenious system of extensions. Each biblical commandment was surrounded by a 'hedge' of minor regulations intended to protect it. So if a Jew was careful to obey the extended law, he was in no danger of breaking the actual biblical Law. This apparently good idea spelled disaster on a number of levels. First, it had the effect of adding to Scripture and in that very act it reduced its authority.

Second, it provided a diversion for debate. The religious Jews began to give as much attention to analysing the extended law as to the holy Law. This again undermined their grasp of the Scripture itself.

Third, it created such a web of impossible demands that ordinary Jews could not cope. They drifted away from the synagogues by the thousand. They had a longing for the God of Israel, but the barrier to belief presented by the religious system was too great for them. So they opted out.

Instead of recognizing that this was the consequence of their own theological embroidery, the religious leaders 'dug in' and accused the people of rejecting the Law and therefore rejecting God. They branded these people 'sinners'.

Ring any bells?

This throws a very different light upon the investment of time which Jesus made in ministering to 'publicans and sinners'. The Gospels frequently show how He met with such people, much to the indignation of the religious.

Publicans (a term which has nothing to do with innkeepers!) were involved with taxation. As such they were involved in the world of business and so were on the edge of religious society – much as men and women in our churches are treated as not quite Grade 1 if they are engaged in what is viewed as 'worldly' professions. Our opinion of career patterns is determined by the degree of 'worldliness' we associate with different jobs. So we see the job of church pastor as much more worthy than that of a bank clerk or traffic warden!

Our use of the word 'sinner' conjures up the idea of someone given to a life of rebellion against God. As we read the Gospels we associate it with thieves, prostitutes and the general 'low-life' of Israel. However, we now see that this is not so. Jesus did not reject *anyone* who came to Him. That is for sure. But He certainly was not identifying with wickedness, nor consorting with thieves and whores.

The phrase 'publicans and sinners' is a reference to the general public, the thousands for whom God remained remote because of the religious system which lay between them and Him. Jesus went out of His way to reach them, and in reaching them He breached the barrier. He hacked it away and brought the love of the Father direct to the people. They *loved* Him for it!

I have decided to follow Jesus

The great need is for us Christians to follow the Lord in His example, not least in this matter of bringing the simplicity of the gospel to those who live around us. It cannot be right for the complexities of the Church to form a barrier to people. How can we expect people to come to our

Saviour if we hedge Him about with all manner of religious gobbledegook?

The way which Jesus opened to the Father is not through the Church. The Church is the community of those who have come to the Father, not the means by which they reach Him. Jesus said, 'I am the way and the truth and the life. No one comes to the Father except through Me' (John 14:6).

Similarly, in Acts 2 we find the straightforward proclamation of the gospel. There is no mention there of any kind of religious requirement beyond the fundamentals leading to personal faith: belief in and acceptance of the truth that Jesus Christ is Lord and Messiah, that He was crucified, buried, raised to life again and taken into heaven. Peter told the inquiring Jews who had, as a result of the preaching, come under conviction that there was need to repent, be baptized and start living a godly life. This they would be able to do because they would receive the power of the Holy Spirit.

The verses which conclude Acts 2 leave us in no doubt that the effect of this simple, yet profound preaching, was that many people from that moment on devoted themselves to Jesus Christ and embraced a lifestyle which was startlingly different from the irreligious *and* the religious communities in which they lived, yet it was what God required.

There is a major difference between the Christianity of the New Testament and the daunting requirements, real or imagined, of the contemporary Church. This is not to cast aspersions, because there are a great many Christians – both leaders and laity – who are doing their level best to cast away the trappings of Christendom and proclaim the true gospel of Jesus Christ. But the general impression given by the Church – especially the leaders of the major denominations – is that the way to God is a tortuous and circuitous path which normal people simply cannot cope with.

The result is a nation filled with seekers after God who cannot find Him. The fault is largely with the Church. May God forgive us ... and the people too.

How well I recall an experience I had when a curate. In those days it was expected that all clergy would wear their clerical collars when out and about in the parish. I followed the fashion. It was especially useful when shopping in town. Queues would evaporate before me as I was ushered to the front! Conversations amongst shoppers would cease instantly and embarrassed smiles turn on me indulgently. The moment I left the shop, normality returned. It used to amuse me greatly. But I came to see that there was nothing funny in it at all.

At a point late on in my curacy we were visited by a Christian who at the time had achieved celebrity status in Evangelical churches because he was a born-again TV actor. Nigel was certainly a character! As I got to know him I was impressed by the simple fact that he was *himself*! What you saw was what you got! No airs, no graces, no projection of image. Lindy and I were fascinated and immensely challenged.

The result of this encounter was that I changed my dress style to something which better expressed *me*. Those were the days of flared jeans and roll-neck sweaters. They became my chosen style instantly. Monday morning saw me down the town making my trendy selection. The local 'His 'n' Hers' hairdresser had a field day, transforming my traditional hairstyle. My vicar – the Revd Canon Ken Prior – was visibly shocked when he saw me at the Tuesday staff meeting, but he tempered his reaction with his usual good grace and we have remained the closest friends through almost thirty years!

I completed my new ensemble by carving a wooden cross, wearing it around my neck on a leather thong.

The point of this story is that there was an instant transformation as regards the reaction of the parishioners to their curate. Instead of embarrassment there were genuine smiles of affection. People no longer seized up in strained silence when I entered a shop: they treated me as if I were normal.

As I began to think about this I was forced to an uncomfortable conclusion. My clerical collar was to the people a symbol of 'the Church', whereas my simple wooden cross was a symbol of Jesus. They had problems with 'the Church', but they wanted to know Jesus. They were demonstrating signs of being classic 'sinners' – just like in Bible days.

I'm so glad the Good News is the same now as it was then!

8
A Tale of Two Cities?

The strong encouragement to anticipate a great revival which forms the centrepiece of many popular preachers' sermons has little or no biblical basis. At any rate, that is my conclusion – and heaven knows I've looked hard enough to find it, being as anxious as the next man to discover that good times are just around the corner.

The truth is that the best possible time *is* coming, but it will be *after* the return of Jesus Christ, when He rules the earth as King of Kings, and not before. There is sufficient in the teaching of Paul and of Jesus Himself to show that difficult times lie immediately ahead, and Christians will need all the faith they can muster to come through them.

Even leaving aside the astonishing events surrounding the death of Diana, Princess of Wales, we live in remarkable days. Natural disasters increase, international unrest is as volatile as ever and internal political and social upheavals signal a breakdown. Crises and challenges to faith in Jesus Christ are all around us. Christians who believe the Bible are regarded by the general public (and by many *in* the churches also) as little better than idiots. Yet I contend that it is *only* the Bible which can enable us to make any sense of life. It also offers the only means whereby we can make any sense of death.

Society is exceedingly complex. People are very different from each other. This is the fascination of studying people. *Vive la difference!* Yet when it comes to addressing people with respect to life and death issues, the Bible preachers and writers seem to concentrate on what we have in common. People are people, whatever.

To Bible preachers, like Paul, we are all rebels against God and need forgiveness. Culture doesn't enter into it – nor do sex, colour, social standing or intellect. King and pauper, guru and murderer, all alike need the salvation which comes only through Jesus Christ and His death on the cross. So the clear, strong declaration of what God is saying today simply *must* be voiced if we are to avoid the shame of seeing great swathes of people being lost eternally through our guilty silence. 'Have mouth, will speak' must be our watchword.

One of the great purposes for which God gave us the Bible is to teach us by example. In it we read about men and women who lived by faith and how they did it is very instructive. For example, how did a man like Paul live prophetically within the culture of his day? He was surrounded by the alien pressures of sophisticated urban life, and yet he maintained a clarity of faith and witness which is legendary.

The prophetic ministry is just as unpopular as it ever was, but the need for it is, if anything, greater. Paul's example (among many others) is extremely helpful to Bible believers as we seek to function prophetically in the period immediately preceding the return of Jesus Christ.

Welcome to Corinth!

When Paul came to the city of Corinth in around 50 AD, it was a salutary experience. Curiously, in spite of our impression that ancient cultures were very different from our own, it seems as if first-century Corinthian life has interesting parallels in twentieth-century western culture. Paul's ministry in Corinth provides us with valuable pointers to our own prophetic ministry in our cities and countryside.

Acts 18 describes Paul coming to Corinth as part of his second apostolic journey. It had been a significant tour of ministry. He had established churches at Philippi, Thessalonica and Berea and had recently come from a fairly frustrating time in Athens (Acts 17:16–34). When he came to Corinth, Paul arrived alone and was apparently very discouraged (see 1 Corinthians 2:3, where he describes his condition as 'in weakness and fear, and with much trembling'). Irrespective of the daunting prospect, Paul evangelized the city for eighteen months. His companions, Silas and Timothy, joined him some time after he had begun his mission.

If you take a look at a map of Greece, you will see that a substantial part of the southern section is virtually an island. It is known as the Peloponnese, and is connected to the mainland by a narrow isthmus, a mere four miles wide. The isthmus formed the sole trading route between the north and south of Greece, and the only link between cities like Athens and Sparta. Corinth is located right at the south end of the isthmus, and so in ancient times it controlled all traffic between north and south.

A further look at the map will indicate that around the southern coast of the Peloponnese, several fingers of land extend into the sea. The tides around this southern coast are extremely treacherous and in Bible times rounding Cape Malea was as terrifying a prospect as later mariners faced when confronting Cape Horn.

Seafarers avoided Cape Malea whenever possible by bridging the isthmus close to Corinth. There were two ports which served the sea traders: one on the western Gulf of Corinth, the other on the eastern Gulf of Saronicus. The western port was called Lechaeum, the eastern port was called Cenchrea. (Cenchrea is mentioned in Acts 18:18, where we find Paul visiting a barber!)

Ships approached either from the west or the east. After docking, their cargoes were unloaded by stevedores and transported by wagon to be reloaded into empty ships on the other side of the isthmus. Smaller vessels were dragged out of the water, set on a conveyor line made of wooden rollers, and then hauled across the four miles from one port to the other, to be relaunched on the other side! The Roman Emperor, Nero, actually contemplated digging a huge canal to connect the two gulfs, but his bold plan was not fulfilled until nearly two thousand years later when Greek engineers sliced their way through.

Commercial traffic poured through ancient Corinth from all directions, so it is easy to understand how the city grew rapidly in power and influence as a major trading centre. Revenue from passing trade made it an enormously wealthy city, and its shifting population created a very cosmopolitan society. F.W. Farrar, the biblical historian, comments in his book, *The Life and Work of St Paul* (Cassell, 1983, p. 401):

Objects of luxury soon found their way to the markets which were visited by every nation in the civilized world. Arabian balsam, Phoenician dates, Libyan ivory, Babylonian carpets, Cilician goat hair, Lyca-onian wool, Phrygian slaves.

Corinth was the 'Vanity Fair' of the ancient world. It was also the home of the Isthmian Games – second only to the Olympic Games in importance. It formed a very large commercial centre: rich, populous, and strategic as a springboard for Paul's evangelism.

Beside its reputation as a commercial capital, Corinth had a reputation for decadence. Its position as a transit city brought thousands of traders and travellers of many kinds and they needed to be entertained. Consequently the pursuit of pleasure had a very high priority in ancient Corinth, and the exploitation of man's baser instincts was indulged to the full. It was so scandalous that a word was coined to describe a person living in drunken and immoral debauchery: such a one was said to be 'corin-thianizing'! The *Chambers English Dictionary* includes a reference to a now obsolete use of the noun 'a Corinth', as meaning 'a brothel'.

Religion in Corinth

There was a deeper, darker reason why Corinth achieved such notoriety in the ancient Greek world. Above the city there towered a great cliff – the Corinthian Acropolis. Here was located a huge temple in honour of Aphrodite, the goddess of love. The worship of Aphrodite as it was enjoyed at Corinth was known throughout the world. The temple employed a thousand priestess/prostitutes. Copulating with one of these girls was believed to be a means of experiencing 'fellowship' with the goddess herself.

It can readily be imagined how many male visitors to Corinth became 'religious' just for their visit, and how many more sought the same activity in a non-religious context! In consequence vice of every description flourished in Corinth. The traders and the sailors revelled in it until the city became a byword for luxury, prosperity, debauchery and filth.

Greeks and Romans

Corinth was built by the Greeks. It was famous for its connection with the sea, and great three-ranked rowing battleships known as 'triremes' were constructed in its massive shipyards. Ancient Corinth was a magnificent city, with stupendous buildings, opulent streets and an aura of sophistication matched only by the degree of its religious corruption.

When Rome rose to power, the pride of the Corinthians led them to form a confederacy with other Greek cities and they refused to respect Roman orders. Rome first defeated the alliance and then in 146 BC General Lucius Mummius led Roman legions to attack Corinth. The proud city was sacked and burned to the ground.

Corinth lay in ruins for exactly one hundred years. In 46 BC, Julius Caesar, realizing its strategic value, supervised its rebuilding as a Roman city. Fine buildings,

enriched with splendid Greek pillars of marble and por-
phyry, embellished with gold and silver which had sur-
vived the conflagration of 146, began to rise side by side
with the wretched hovels of wood and mud plaster in
which lived the mass of the poorer population. Corinth
rapidly regained its old importance as a commercial centre, but now as the Roman provincial capital of Achaia.

Corinth was settled by veterans from the Roman
armies and merchants moved in once more – peoples
from every corner of the civilized world. A large contin-
gent of Jews settled there, and by the time Paul arrived in
around 50 AD, the Jews had established at least one synagogue building in the city. This is referred to in Acts 18:4:
'Every Sabbath he reasoned in the synagogue, trying to
persuade Jews and Greeks.'

Roman Corinth quickly regained its old notoriety. F.W.
Farrar (*op cit.* p. 401–402) speaks of 'this mongrel and
heterogeneous population of Greek adventurers, Roman
bourgeois, with a tainting infusion of Phoenicians; this
mass of Jews, ex-soldiers, philosophers, merchants,
sailors, freedmen, slaves, trades people, hucksters and
agents of every form of vice.' William Barclay, in his book
The Letters to the Corinthians (St Andrew Press, 1954, p. 4),
comments:

> Remember the background of Corinth, remember
> its name for wealth and luxury, for drunkenness and
> immorality and vice, for the nameless and the shame-
> less things and then read 1 Corinthians 6:9–11:
>
> '... neither the sexually immoral nor idolaters
> nor adulterers, nor male prostitutes, nor homosexual
> offenders, nor thieves, nor the greedy, nor drunkards,

nor slanderers, nor swindlers will inherit the Kingdom of God. *And that is what some of you were ...'.*

The remarkable thing is that in this unlikely place, the
apostle Paul invested eighteen months of his life and ministry. Some of his greatest work was done here, and many
people were saved.

Paul, man about town

We are dependent upon seventeen verses in Acts 18 to
give us the whole story of a year and a half's hard work in
Corinth! Fortunately, Luke (the writer of Acts) tells us
quite a lot about it.

When Paul arrived in Corinth from Athens he lodged
with a Jewish couple named Aquila and Priscilla. It seems
as though he knew them, or knew of them. They, like Paul,
were tent makers by trade. The Greek word *skenopoios* can
also mean 'leather worker'. The making of sandals, belts,
bags and tunics would easily lend itself to irregular working 'on the hoof', whereas the making of tents would
require a more settled environment.

Aquila and Priscilla formerly lived in Rome, but they
were forced out by the emperor Claudius as a result of
Jewish rioting in the capital. In consequence of this
edict of Claudius, Jews scattered far and wide into
provincial cities and towns where they re-established
themselves.

Paul followed his normal plan and began ministering
at the synagogue. Trouble arose on account of his preaching, so he left the synagogue and started a house-meeting

next door. One of Paul's early successes was the conversion of the leader of the synagogue himself, an event which did little to endear Paul to the rest of the Jews!

Shortly after Paul began his preaching in Corinth, a new Roman governor of Achaia was appointed. His name was Lucius Junius Annaeus Gallio. His father and brother, both named Seneca, were noted for their powers of rhetoric and philosophy. By all contemporary accounts Gallio was something of a rarity among highly placed Roman officials for he was noted as a man of refinement and fairness – unusual qualities in men who normally held such office!

In the light of Paul's effective ministry, the furious Jews tried to take advantage of Gallio, and they attempted to get his ban placed upon Paul. Wise Gallio saw through their ploy, and refused to take up the case. Because of this Paul was able to continue the work of establishing the Corinthian church before moving on into Syria some months later.

Doing as the Romans did?

The story of man is one of rising and falling empires. They come and they go – Egypt, Assyria, Babylon, Persia, Greece, Rome ... each has its little day and then is forced by another to leave the stage. Historians catalogue what they consider to be the reasons for the demise of great empires. There is often a remarkable similarity between them, leaving us with the uncomfortable thought that, as was said earlier, if we do not learn from the mistakes of history, we are doomed to repeat them.

Edward Gibbon, the eighteenth-century English historian of the Roman period, who wrote a monumental work, *The Decline and Fall of the Roman Empire*, provided a list of what he considered to be the reasons for the demise of the Roman Empire after the second century. These were characteristics of Roman life which ultimately grew to choke it to death, but the seeds were in evidence within the culture Paul faced in Roman Corinth in the early 50s.

There was a decline in personal morality: family life was undermined with the rise of homosexuality and the rapid increase in divorce. The pursuit of pleasure became an obsession, and entertainment was filled with violence, nudity and perversions of every kind. Financial demands on the imperial exchequer to fund extravagant social programmes meant steeply increasing taxation which became unbearable. Huge sums were continually being spent on maintaining the Roman war machine. Religious pluralism, encouraged to draw the disparate elements in the Empire together, served only to create a society obsessed with superstition and fear.

Such observations are extraordinary in their parallels with contemporary western culture. London life today has fascinating features which it shares with first-century Corinth. Paul was singularly successful in his mission to Corinth, so perhaps the ministry of Paul to the Corinthians can provide valuable insights into the type of message we Christians need to bring to our own society. What was Paul's message?

The gospel according to Paul

What was his evangelism like? Was it the same sort of thing that we hear at modern evangelistic rallies? What *is* the gospel according to St. Paul?

In order to discover the content of Paul's evangelism in Corinth, we need to examine Acts 18, where it is chronicled, and his first letter to the Corinthians which he wrote two years later, in which he makes many references to it. Acts 18:5 sums up Paul's activities in Corinth in a very direct statement, 'Paul devoted himself exclusively to preaching, testifying to the Jews that Jesus was the Christ.'

His textbook could only be the Old Testament because that is the only source of authority acceptable to Jews. Paul made the Corinthian synagogue his primary evangelistic platform until he was refused permission to preach there. He then went to a nearby house and continued his preaching to a wider audience. But his gospel message was extremely clear: he preached and testified that Jesus was the Messiah (Christ).

This was Paul's method right from the start of his ministry. Acts 9:20 and 22 make it plain that after his personal encounter with the risen Jesus on the road to Damascus and his subsequent baptism in the Holy Spirit in the city, Paul's preaching went through a metamorphosis. From being one who totally discounted Jesus' claims he became convinced that Jesus *is* the Christ! Paul immediately began preaching this in the Damascus synagogue, much to the astonishment and consternation of many of the Jews. Paul's method of evangelism was to keep it simple. In 1 Corinthians 2:1 he writes,

> When I came to you, brothers, I did not come with eloquence or superior wisdom as I proclaimed to you the testimony about God. For I resolved to know nothing while I was with you except Jesus Christ and Him crucified ... my message and my preaching were not with wise and persuasive words but with a demonstration of the Spirit's power, so that your faith might not rest on men's wisdom but on God's power.

So as Paul confronted the culture of Corinth, his approach was not one of compromise! He was not intent on making his message palatable. His one motive was to speak the truth, the whole truth and nothing but the truth, no matter what it cost.

The effect of Paul's simple gospel presentation was impressive. Acts 18:8 indicates that many Corinthians – Jews and Gentiles – believed and were baptized. Paul preached the truth about *Jesus Christ,* based upon the Old Testament Scriptures. They *believed* in the Lord and were *baptized.*

If we compare 1 Corinthians 1:23 with 2:2 and 15:1–4 we discover further details concerning Paul's preaching about Jesus. It is clear that in spite of knowing he would meet with hostility, he placed the emphasis unswervingly upon Christ's crucifixion and its unique power in bringing salvation to the world:

> We preach Christ crucified: a stumbling block to Jews and foolishness to Gentiles.

> For I resolved to know nothing while I was with you except Jesus Christ and Him crucified.

Now, brothers, I want to remind you of the gospel I preached to you, which you received and on which you have taken your stand. By this gospel you are saved, if you hold firmly to the word I preached to you. Otherwise you have believed in vain. For what I received I passed on to you as of first importance: that Christ died for our sins according to the Scriptures, that He was buried, that He was raised on the third day according to the Scriptures.

Although it was a stumbling block to Jews and foolishness to Greeks (Gentiles), Paul's resolution was to know nothing while in Corinth 'except *Jesus Christ and Him crucified*'.

In 1 Corinthians 15:1 Paul made it clear that the Corinthians did not merely give mental acknowledgement to the message which was announced to them, they *received it* and *took their stand on it*. It is one thing to acknowledge the truth of something, it is quite another to accept the consequences of it and make it the basis of life. Receiving the gospel is accepting Jesus Christ as Saviour and Lord, and taking one's stand on it is living in complete faith and trust of Jesus Christ.

Paul said that the 'gospel' which he proclaimed, and which had power to save the Corinthians, comprised three elements:

- Christ died for our sins according to the Scriptures;
- He was buried;
- He was raised on the third day according to the Scriptures.

Fitting these elements together with the other references to Paul's 'gospel' given above, his evangelistic message emerges.

- Jesus Christ is Messiah (Christ) and Lord
- He died on the cross according to the Scriptures
- He rose from the dead
- In order to appropriate this message a response is required:
  Receive the truth by accepting Jesus Christ as Saviour and Lord
  Take your stand by faith in Him
  Be baptized in water.

In reconstructing Paul's gospel we must add two further elements which he includes as essential.

First, in 1 Corinthians 2:4, 5 he describes his preaching in Corinth as being with a 'demonstration of the Spirit's power', and not mere words. Furthermore, he describes the Christians as not lacking 'any spiritual gift' (1:2), and devotes a long section in his letter (chapters 12 to 14) to advising them how to use these gifts of the Holy Spirit. Quite clearly they had received what the Bible calls 'the Baptism in the Holy Spirit'.

Second, in 1 Corinthians 1:2 he defines 'the church' as being people who are 'sanctified in Christ Jesus and called to be holy'. In 3:17 Paul actually compares Christians with a temple – God's holy living area! The implication is clear – Christians are to be holy in every area of life.

Fitting all this together we can see clearly that this is what Paul preached about in Corinth. He elected not to appeal to the people through their own culture or to look for what was commendable in their traditional religious systems. On the contrary, he declared the simple truth, as he saw it, with no hint of compromise.

- Jesus is Messiah (Christ) and Lord
- He died on the cross according to the Scriptures
- He rose from the dead
- In order to appropriate this message a response is required:
  Receive the truth by accepting Jesus Christ as Saviour and Lord
  Take your stand by faith in Him
  Be baptized in water
  Be baptized in the Holy Spirit
  Live a holy life.

This analysis is far more important than we may realize. It is not merely Paul's idea of evangelism, it is *biblical* evangelism! This means it is truly *the gospel according to the Bible*! But to make such a claim, we need more evidence.

'Call the next witness!'

In Acts 18:7 we are told that when Paul left the Corinthian synagogue and began preaching next door, it was at the invitation of a man named Titius Justus – a Roman name. Titius Justus is called a 'worshipper of God' which presumably means he had been attending the Jewish synagogue. He now left the synagogue in order to provide Paul with a preaching platform in his home. Quite clearly Paul's preaching brought swift results among the Gentile population and Acts 18:8 says, 'many of the Corinthians who heard him believed and were baptized'.

Corinth was a cosmopolitan city with a huge Gentile population. It was essentially a Gentile city. An interesting question arises when we compare one city mission with another. Was the gospel preached to Gentiles any different from that preached to Jews? If it was, we would have to conclude that cultural factors affect it, and the truth in one situation is not the same as truth in another. However, if we discover that the gospel to the Gentiles is exactly the same as that preached to the Jews we have a powerful argument for saying there is only *one* gospel, whatever the situation we are addressing.

The clearest example of gospel preaching in an almost exclusively Jewish situation is the ministry of Peter at the Jewish Feast of Pentecost in the city of Jerusalem seven weeks after our Lord's resurrection.

Peter in Jerusalem

A careful reading of Acts 2, with Paul's gospel outline beside us, provides us with a remarkable comparison. Peter's preaching to Jews in Jerusalem is exactly the same as Paul's to Gentiles in Corinth! *The gospel to the Jews is identical with the gospel to the Gentiles*. This is not a coincidence. Peter's gospel and Paul's gospel are identical because both proclaimed the *biblical gospel*!

Here is my analysis of the evangelistic preaching of Peter as we find it in Acts 2, but slotted into Paul's outline as we extracted it from Acts 18 and from the First Letter to the Corinthians:

- Jesus is Messiah and Lord (Acts 2:36)
- He died on the cross according to the Scriptures (Acts 2:23)
  He rose from the dead (Acts 2:24–32)
- In order to appropriate this message a response is required:
  Receive the truth by accepting Jesus Christ as Saviour and Lord (Acts 2:41)
  Take your stand by faith in Him (Acts 2:38, 44)
  Be baptized in water (Acts 2:38, 41)
  Be baptized in the Holy Spirit (Acts 2:38)
  Live a holy life (Acts 2:40)

One of the basic principles of Bible interpretation is the principle of 'first mention'. The first mention of a theme or doctrine in the Bible is extremely vital and forms a keynote statement which should govern all subsequent references to it.

Acts 2 is the 'first mention' of *evangelism by born-again believers in the power of the Holy Spirit*. So the example of evangelistic proclamation we have demonstrated here is the keynote statement which should govern any other expression of evangelism. Here is God's 'blueprint'. It should not surprise us, therefore, to find that Paul's evangelistic preaching and ministry at Corinth mirrored so precisely Peter's in Acts 2! They both got it from the same source – God Himself!

I cannot overstate the importance of this. If this is truly the biblical gospel, then it follows that nothing can be added to it and nothing taken away. Any attempt to do either results in a *different gospel* resulting in all manner of problems. The most serious is the assumption that because a person has heard a version of the gospel and responded to it, he or she must therefore be a true Christian.

But if the gospel preached is not the true gospel, any resulting decisions are based upon false premises and are therefore lacking in varying degrees. In some cases the lack may well be disastrous, building upon false hope a 'faith' which is based upon presumption rather than truth. The responsibility for such false gospel preaching lies with Christians and nowhere else. Ours is the responsibility to speak the truth, the whole truth and *nothing* but the truth.

There is one gospel, and only one. Paul preached it in Corinth, Peter in Jerusalem. This provides us with clear guidelines for evangelism which should not be tampered with. Whatever our cultural setting the gospel remains unchanged and unchanging.

The unchanging gospel

The word 'gospel' is the Greek *evangelion*, meaning 'good news'. But it is good news of a particular kind. When Greek armies went to war, much was at stake. Victory ensured freedom for the people, while defeat meant slavery and death. We can imagine the eagerness with which people awaited news of the battle. Would messengers from the front bring news of defeat or of victory?

Picture the scene. A runner is seen approaching. The people run to meet him, knowing that he has news of the battle. His gasped cry is enough to send the people into paroxysms of joy – '*EVANGELION*!' – 'It is good news of *victory*!'

Here, then, is the meaning of 'gospel'. It is much more than good news. It is not the word Greeks would have used to say, 'I have some good news – tomorrow is a public holiday!' The emphasis is very much upon good news of a great *victory* over a vicious enemy. Its use by the New Testament writers is obvious. The foundation of our gospel is the good news of Christ's victory over sin and death. It is 'Jesus Christ and Him crucified', just as Paul describes in 1 Corinthians 2:2.

For many people, Bible-based Christianity is unacceptable because of its insistence upon certain 'impossible' events. The virgin birth, God becoming man, the crucifixion and resurrection of Jesus are but four. Yet traditional Christian belief has always demanded acceptance of these difficult tenets. To have jettisoned them in ages past would surely have opened the door to millions of would-be converts, who admire greatly the moral base of our faith and its emphasis upon forgiveness and love. Jesus Himself has always been a figure of the highest admiration and affection, and so it would make perfect sense to strip the Christian faith of its dogmatic insistence upon events in His life which are so far-fetched. That is certainly the view of many today, so-called Christians among them.

The very fact that in the face of the most virulent attacks, there has been throughout Christian history a determined remnant who held to these fundamental tenets of faith should give pause for thought. Could it be that they are true? Could it be that without them the Christian faith is destroyed? I believe passionately that it is so, no matter how much the battle rages in my mind. If my thinking is at variance with the clear teaching of the Bible, it is my thinking which must change.

A TALE OF TWO CITIES?

When writing to his friends in Corinth, Paul took a very strong line with regard to the crucifixion and the physical resurrection of Jesus. Not for him the bleating compromise which views these matters as some kind of 'spiritual' reality as against hard physical fact!

As regards the resurrection, 1 Corinthians 15 is one continuous and crystal clear defence of bodily resurrection – particularly that of Jesus Christ. Within that chapter Paul doesn't mince his words! For example, 1 Corinthians 15:12–19, which is so clear that it is worth quoting in full:

> But if it is preached that Christ has been raised from the dead, how can some of you say that there is no resurrection of the dead? If there is no resurrection of the dead, then not even Christ has been raised. And *if Christ has not been raised, our preaching is useless and so is your faith*. More than that, we are then found to be false witnesses about God that He raised Christ from the dead. But He did not raise Him if in fact the dead are not raised. For if the dead are not raised, then Christ is not raised either. *And if Christ is not raised, your faith is futile; you are still dead in your sins*. Then those also who have fallen asleep in Christ are lost. *If only for this life we have hope in Christ, we are to be pitied more than all men*.

That is pretty clear! In order to have a resurrection there must have been a death. And it is essential that we seek an understanding of what took place when Jesus died on the cross. If Jesus did not die and rise again, the Christian faith has no credibility or even reason to be.

The body of Jesus Christ which came *from* the tomb on the morning of resurrection was the same that was placed *in* the tomb the evening after the crucifixion. And yet Paul says that in certain senses it was altered. It had undergone a number of dramatic changes, but it was *not* a replacement body, it was the same one. The historical details provided by the Gospel writers confirm this. They talk about the crucifixion scars still on the body of the risen Lord: 'Why do doubts rise in your minds? [said Jesus] Look at My *hands* and My *feet*' (Luke 24:38, 39).

John makes a great deal of the encounter between Jesus and His disciple, Thomas, which took place after the resurrection: 'Then He said to Thomas, "Put your finger here; see my *hands*. Reach out your hand and put it into my *side*. Stop doubting and believe"' (John 20:27).

Revelation 5:6 is a great statement regarding Jesus Christ in heaven: 'Then I saw a Lamb, *looking* as if it had been *slain* ...' How would the Lamb (Jesus) *look* as if it had been killed? The only answer can be that it carried the marks of its death which were clearly visible.

In 1 Corinthians 15, Paul makes it abundantly clear that true believers in Christ will rise after their death as He rose after His. The body that goes to the grave is the *same one* that is reconstituted at resurrection. But in verses 42–53 Paul lists six alterations to the body which God effects before it is raised up again.

- Our present body is perishable, the resurrection body will be imperishable.
- Our present body dies in dishonour, the resurrection body is raised in honour.

- Our present body is weak, the resurrection body is powerful.
- Our present body is natural, the resurrection body is spiritual.
- Our present body is like Adam (a natural man), the resurrection body is like Christ (the heavenly man).
- Our present body is mortal, the resurrection body is immortal.

Quite clearly any evidence of disease or mutilation due to accident or conflict will be made good in our resurrection body, and yet if we have sustained wounds as a consequence of our witness as Christians, those will remain, not as blemishes but as adornments, testifying to our devotion to Christ. It is confident hope in the resurrection of the dead through faith in Jesus Christ which enables the Christian to throw himself completely at the feet of the Lord and to maintain a deep joy even when all hell appears to break out around him.

Those who seek to destroy the gospel of Jesus Christ have always done so by attacking His crucifixion and resurrection. They either insinuate that He did not actually die on the cross and that the whole episode was a gigantic hoax perpetrated by his supporters, or else they deny his coming back to life again as a further elaborate hoax. In fact, it must be one or the other. We are either dealing with historical facts or we are dealing with fairy stories.

Is the New Testament reliable?

It is fashionable among those who wish to denigrate the New Testament to suggest that the documents are not historically reliable. Because they were written so long ago, the New Testament books must, it is claimed, have been altered substantially by followers of Jesus who wanted to make Him out as a God-man. So references to His death and resurrection, for example, have been carefully inserted into the text by those wishing to create the doctrine.

This is entirely wishful thinking on the part of sceptics. Ancient writers and historians like Flavius Josephus (who was born four years after the crucifixion) refer to Jesus dying on the cross. And as far as the New Testament itself is concerned, we know perfectly well by means of textual criticism what the original writers actually wrote.

In earlier centuries, before the advent of printing, copies of manuscripts were made entirely by hand. In regard to authenticating ancient writings, the more copies we have, the more confident we can be as to the actual text. Professor F.F. Bruce (formerly Rylands Professor of Biblical Criticism and Exegesis at Manchester University) shows in his book *Are the New Testament Documents Reliable?* (Eerdmans, 1954) how rich the New Testament is in the vast amount of documental evidence which exists when compared with accepted non-biblical documents from the ancient past.

The earliest existing manuscript of the great Greek writer Herodotus dates from 900 AD. Eight copies have been found. Also from around 900 AD we have the earliest copy of Thucydides. Seven later copies have been found. Caesar's Gallic War was written around 50 BC, but the earliest of the ten copies found dates from 900 AD. Livy's Roman History, written at the start of the first century AD, was unknown until 900 AD. Twenty copies have been found. Tacitus wrote around 100 AD. Twenty copies of his work also exist, the earliest dating from 1100 AD.

Although a large interval exists between the date of writing and the earliest copies found, and very few copies have actually been discovered, respectable classical scholars accept the authenticity of these works and consider them reliable history.

When we turn to the New Testament the situation is entirely different. Many of these same scholars appear to adopt a completely different attitude: they pour scorn upon the New Testament documents and ridicule those who accept their historicity despite the enormous wealth of material we possess.

There are excellent full manuscripts of the New Testament dating from 350 AD, only 250 years after the last of the documents was written. Many part documents from this period exist and one fragment of John's Gospel dates from before 150 AD! There are over 5,000 Greek manuscripts of the New Testament and 10,000 in Latin. Over 9,000 manuscripts exist in other languages and there are over 36,000 references to New Testament writings in the works of the early church fathers.

Ignoring this overwhelming deluge of authenticating evidence can only be ascribed to vested interest. To admit that the New Testament is historically accurate and true demands a response of faith, which is probably why so many 'scholars' are reluctant to acknowledge the truth. One of the foremost biblical critics, F.J.A. Hort, said, 'In the variety and fullness of the evidence on which it rests, the text of the New Testament stands absolutely and unapproachably alone among ancient prose writings' (*The New Testament in the Original Greek*, Macmillan, New York, vol. 1, p. 561).

Sir Frederic G. Kenyon, the great Greek manuscript scholar, in his book *The Bible and Archaeology* (Harper and Row, 1940), wrote:

> The interval then between the dates of original composition and the earliest extant evidence becomes so small as to be in fact negligible, and the last foundation for any doubt that the Scriptures have come down to us substantially as they were written has now been removed. Both the *authenticity* and the *general integrity* of the books of the New Testament may be regarded as finally established.

9
Paul and the Cross
of Jesus

Paul's insistence upon preaching about the crucifixion when he was faced with the daunting prospect of evangelizing Corinth, is a powerful indicator that it needs to form the heart of our evangelism also, whatever our cultural setting.

In 1 Corinthians 1:17–18, Paul insists that 'Christ did not send me to baptize, but to preach the gospel – not with words of human wisdom, lest the cross of Christ be emptied of its power. For the message of the cross is foolishness to those who are perishing, but to us who are being saved it is the power of God.'

If Paul had preached clever ideas and concepts instead of the gospel, the cross of Christ would have been emptied of its power and so his preaching would have been ineffective for salvation, no matter how acceptable it might be to the rational mind. The power of God is the message of the cross of Christ and not any other, however plausible it may sound.

A little later on in the chapter (verses 20–25) Paul makes it clear that he was not prepared to play the religious or philosophical games demanded by Jewish and Greek society. People around him were anxious to see impressive miracles and to hear cleverly devised ideas and theories, but Paul would have none of it. He faced the jeering scorn of his critics, refusing to give them what they wanted. He simply preached Christ crucified. Paul refused to temper his message in order to make it appealing or acceptable or respectable. As far as he was concerned, he would preach only the biblical gospel with no addition, subtraction or substitution.

Paul's basic gospel message was not only the foundation of his evangelism, it was also the basis for his entire teaching programme. In addressing the problems of the church at Corinth, Paul reminded his friends about the power by which they were saved, and in which they were to live – the power of the cross of Christ.

Paul had been ministering in Athens immediately before coming to Corinth. It was at Athens, probably for the only time in his ministry, that Paul had attempted to convey the gospel by relating it to certain aspects of their own religion and even quoting Greek authorities. Acts 17:22–31 contains his famous sermon preached in Athens, and serves as something of a warning to Christian preachers not to try to 'mix it' with fashionable ideas of the day. Although everything he said was true, Paul's sermon to the members of the great debating society of the day (the Areopagites) cannot be compared with the crystal clarity of his preaching in Corinth. It is interesting that Luke's comment on Paul's ministry in Athens (Acts 17:34) is decidedly muted: 'A few men became followers of Paul and believed. Among them was Dionysius, a member of the Areopagus, also a woman named Damaris and a number of others.'

It would seem that Paul decided then and there he

would *never* make that mistake again! Whoever his hearers were, however lowly, however exalted, however simple, however clever, his message would ever and only be the simple yet profound message of Jesus Christ and Him crucified. He came on to Corinth with that conviction burning in his heart.

The crucifixion of Jesus is the central point of history. It is the crux of the matter as far as God and the Bible are concerned. Everything that precedes it in the Scriptures points forward to the cross, and everything that follows it points back to it.

The cross in the Bible

When Paul speaks of the cross, it is not the cross itself he is thinking of, it is the *cross event* – the crucifixion; the shedding of the blood of Jesus; His suffering and death to redeem mankind. The focal point at the crucifixion is the Man *on* the cross, not the cross itself.

Some people wear crosses, bow to crosses and have crosses hanging in their homes. But if there is no recognition of the Man *on* the cross, and what He did there, such an object is a mere token of superstition, no better than an amulet or charm.

During former ages supposed pieces of the cross on which Jesus died were venerated as very powerful objects of devotion. This is true today in many parts of the world where Christianity is mingled with superstition. Such artefacts are known as 'relics'. Other relics include personal belongings of the 'saints' and even bits of their physical bodies! It was common during the Middle Ages for relics to be installed beneath the altars of pre-Reformation churches and cathedrals. These were (and in some cases still are) treated with such veneration that they became objects of worship in themselves.

All over the world there are Catholic churches which are believed to possess pieces of the cross on which Our Lord was crucified. It is an intriguing fact that these pieces are so numerous that put together they would create a 'cross' of gigantic proportions! It is to be regretted, perhaps, that the cross has become such a universal symbol of our faith. A hideous Roman gibbet should not be the focus, rather than the precious Saviour who died upon it.

For Paul, a man with a thoroughly Orthodox Jewish background and a thoroughly Christian 'foreground', the crucifixion of Jesus was the perfect fulfilment of Old Testament Scripture. So many 'types' from the Old Testament were fulfilled by Jesus when He died on the cross: for example, the Passover Lamb of Exodus 12 (applied to Jesus in 1 Corinthians 5:7) and the Suffering Servant of Isaiah 52 and 53 (applied to Jesus by Paul in Philippians 2:7 and by Philip in Acts 8:32–35).

Theologically, the word 'cross' was used by the New Testament writers to summarize the whole work of redemption, when Christ died for our sin. Paul uses the word 'cross' in this sense in 1 Corinthians. Take, for example, chapter 1:17ff, where 'cross' clearly stands for the whole work of redemption through Our Lord's atoning death.

If the 'Diana Prophecy' is an indication that the time has arrived for an all-out drive to bring the good news of Jesus Christ's victory on the cross to our people, we need a clear grasp of the facts about the death of our Saviour.

The cross as a tool of Roman execution

Surprisingly, two millennia of devotion to Jesus and His death have to some extent blunted the sharpness of crucifixion in the minds of Christians. It is all too easy to see it through the eyes of sculptors and painters, who in creating objects to aid devotion have created works of art rather than of realism, of beauty rather than hideousness, of pathos rather than shameful, foul humiliation. Crucifixion was a vile means of torturing a man to death. It involved the complete exposure of the victim to public humiliation and lingering, agonizing death by suffocation.

The word normally translated 'cross' is *stauros*, or crucifying 'post'. These posts, like stumpy telegraph poles about seven feet in height, were normally driven into the ground in groups by the side of main roads. They remained in position to act as a permanent deterrent to lawbreakers.

A man sentenced to death by crucifixion was made to shoulder a piece of heavy timber, some six feet in length, and carry it from the place of sentencing to the place of execution. Once there Roman soldiers would strip him completely and tie or nail the victim's hands to the piece of timber, lifting it on to a fixing point on top of the vertical post. The legs of the man would be doubled up tightly under him and the feet fastened to the post by tying or nailing.

The Gospels indicate that Jesus was nailed to the cross, not tied. The appalling agony involved in this inhuman treatment was compounded by the fact that such a position – sagging from the horizontal timber with arms outstretched – constricted the ribs, preventing breathing.

The only way breaths could be snatched was if the victim pushed himself up on his feet in order to expand his lungs. When we remember that the feet were often nailed, we can scarcely imagine the searing agony of such a movement. But it was essential every time a breath was required. Alternating between taking His weight on His nailed feet or hands and fighting for breath, Jesus suffered in this fashion for six hours from 9 am until 3 pm. For Christians the wonder of it is that Jesus suffered such a death as our substitute.

Sometimes if time was pressing, the Romans could hasten the death of a crucified man by breaking his legs. The effect of this was obvious. It prevented him from heaving himself up to breathe, and so death by suffocation came swiftly. With Jesus, the Romans considered breaking His legs because it was getting late in the day. John 19:31–33 says:

Now it was the day of Preparation, and the next day was to be a special Sabbath. Because the Jews did not want the bodies left on the crosses during the Sabbath, they asked Pilate [the Roman Governor] to have the legs broken and the bodies taken down. The soldiers therefore came and broke the legs of the first man who had been crucified with Jesus, and then those of the other. But when they came to Jesus and found that He was already dead, they did not break His legs.

This was an extraordinary fulfilment of an Old Testament passage which refers to the killing of Passover lambs. It was forbidden to break the bones of the lamb, and in this as in many other parallels, we are shown that Jesus Christ is the true Passover Lamb of which all others were mere types.

The effect of the crucifixion

In Colossians 1:19–20, Paul speaks about peace with God being re-established through the blood Jesus shed on the cross. This is a reference to His death. The death of Jesus has brought to an end the terrible hostility which existed between man and God which resulted from the Fall. This is very good news! No wonder the New Testament writers continually use the word *evangelion* to describe it. Jesus Christ has won the greatest victory of all the ages: He has conquered sin and death on our behalf!

People often ask why we Christians make so much of the crucifixion of Jesus. After all, His death on a cross was scarcely unique. The Romans crucified thousands of men all over the Empire. Perhaps it is because Jesus was *nailed* to His cross? But skeletal remains have been discovered from the Roman period with clear evidence of nailing through the hands and feet. So what makes the death of Christ different?

To reach into the depths of this question to find an answer, we must appeal once more to Paul's ministry to Corinth. In 2 Corinthians 5:21, Paul says that God the Father made Jesus to *be sin* for us, so that *in Him* we might become the *righteousness of God.* The consequences of this are as vast as the immeasurable grace of God!

Paul says that when Our Lord hung on the cross, He identified with our sin to such a degree that He carried

God's judgement for the sin of the entire world. This was not only for His contemporaries but also for the millions of people who lived before 33 AD and those who have lived since. But what does it mean to say as Paul says, 'God made Him who had no sin to be sin for us, so that in Him we might become the righteousness of God'? Here is what we might term 'The Royal Exchange'. Our Lord Jesus Christ took on my personal sin and all its foul consequences leading to death, in order that I might take on His personal righteousness and all its glorious consequences leading to eternal life!

One of the extraordinary things about the Bible is the way it focuses upon Jesus Himself. Although it sounds strange, He is actually the central theme in both Old and New Testaments. In Luke 24:27 we have a reference to Jesus speaking with two believers who had left Jerusalem and were making their way home following the crucifixion. The risen Jesus joined them as they walked and his conversation with them changed utter desolation into profound joy! 'And beginning with Moses and all the Prophets, Jesus explained to them what was said in all the Scriptures concerning Himself.' This can only apply to the *Old* Testament.

Similarly in Luke 24:44 we find the risen Lord speaking with His disciples: 'He said to them, "This is what I told you while I was still with you: everything must be fulfilled that is written about Me in the Law of Moses, the Prophets and the Psalms."' The titles 'The Law of Moses, the Prophets and the Psalms' embrace the entire contents of the Hebrew Scriptures. So Jesus is indicating that the Old Testament is packed with revelation about Him, not least in His suffering.

A classic example is Isaiah 52:13 through to the end of chapter 53. This puzzling passage appears to be Messianic, and yet it describes appalling suffering. This did not fit the Messianic expectations of the Jews and the passage was a bone of much contention among the rabbis. It was this kind of passage to which Jesus referred the couple on the road to Emmaus and also His disciples. His Messianic suffering would precede His Messianic glory.

Isaiah 52:13 through to the end of chapter 53 is the passage which features in Acts 8, where Philip is led to open the Scriptures to the Ethiopian Chancellor. Acts 8:32–33 shows that the Ethiopian was reading from Isaiah 53 and could not understand whom it was about. Philip, under inspiration of the Holy Spirit, showed him that it referred to Jesus dying on the cross: 'Then Philip began with that very passage of Scripture and told him the good news about Jesus.'

So here in Isaiah is a prophetic description of Our Lord's appalling suffering as He died on the cross. In this it is remarkably graphic, giving astonishing insights into what actually took place when Jesus Our Saviour took upon Himself all the horror of our sin.

This takes us to the heart of the matter. Here is the reason why the crucifixion of Jesus Christ is utterly unique. He is the only person ever to become sin with the sin of the whole world and to suffer death in order to bring salvation to humanity. Only He could do it – and He did it! But the cost was unbelievable. This is the prophet's description in Isaiah 52:14 and 53:2:

> His appearance was so disfigured, beyond that of any man and His form marred beyond human likeness.

He had no beauty or majesty to attract us to Him, nothing in His appearance that we should desire Him.

Why, we may ask, was His carrying of our sin such a ghastly business that it disfigured Jesus so grotesquely? The answer is to be found in understanding the Hebrew words in the verses that follow the above quotations. Here is Isaiah 53:3–6. Note the emphases.

He was despised and rejected by men, a man of *pains* and familiar with *sicknesses*. Like one from whom men hide their faces, He was despised and we esteemed Him not. Surely He took up our *sicknesses* and carried our *pains*, yet we considered Him *stricken by God, smitten by Him and afflicted*.

But He was pierced for *our* transgressions, He was crushed for *our* iniquities; the punishment that brought *us* peace was upon *Him*, and by *His* stripes *we* are healed.

We all, like sheep, have gone astray, each of us has turned to his own way; and *the Lord has laid on Him the iniquity of us all*.

In verses 7 to 12, Isaiah writes,

He was oppressed and afflicted ... From arrest and judgement He was taken away ... cut off from the land of the living; for the transgression of my people He was stricken ...Yet it was the Lord's will to crush Him and *make Him sick* ... the Lord makes His life a guilt offering ... my Righteous Servant will justify many, and He will bear their iniquities ... He poured out His life unto death, and was numbered with the transgressors. For He bore the sin of many, and made intercession for the transgressors.

In these terrible, yet wonderful verses, Isaiah presents us with the stark truth about what it meant for Jesus to become sin for mankind. In His dear body and mind He took all the sin, pain, wounds, sickness, disease, depression and suffering for us all. His body was just a mass of putrefying flesh – foul, stinking, unrecognizable. Such a spectacle is almost beyond imagination. It would doubtless have been totally overwhelming for the unveiled gaze of anyone except the Father Himself. Could it be a mark of His infinite grace that He blotted out the scene from all eyes but His own by sending darkness to cover the whole earth (see Matthew 27:45)?

Paul's understanding of all this would have been profound. Small wonder, therefore, that he is convinced that the cross of Christ is the complete answer to all the difficulties confronting the Christians at Corinth! It is the complete answer for Britain, and it is the only one.

As I write this essay, it is particularly poignant for me because I have just learned that my dear father is dying of pancreatic cancer. Death is staring us in the face. And yet that ghastly spectre is shattered by the greater wonder that Jesus Christ carried my father's sin and all its foul consequences in His body on the cross, and one day soon my dad will fly into the arms of his Saviour, made righteous with his Saviour's righteousness. Indeed, as Paul caught it so perfectly in 1 Corinthians 1:18, *to us who are being saved, the message of the cross is the power of God*!

The great seventeenth-century German hymn writer, Paul Gerhardt, wrote a wonderful hymn, which seems to encapsulate so much of Paul's sense of awe at the cross-event at Calvary.

O Sacred Head, sore wounded, with grief and shame
   weighed down!
O Kingly Head, surrounded with thorns, Thine only
   crown!
How pale art Thou with anguish, with sore abuse and
   scorn!
How does that visage languish, which once was bright
   as morn!

O Lord of life and glory, what bliss 'til now was Thine!
I read the wondrous story; I joy to call Thee mine.
Thy grief and bitter passion were all for sinners' gain;
Mine, mine was the transgression, but Thine the deadly
   pain.

What language shall I borrow to praise Thee, heavenly
   Friend,
For this Thy dying sorrow, Thy pity without end?
Lord, make me Thine for ever, nor let me faithless prove;
O let me never, never abuse such dying love.

10
Look Out – or
Look Out!

The apostle Paul was nothing if not forthright! He was not one to mince his words. His concern to preach the gospel and to encourage other believers to do so is writ large in all his letters. In Romans 10:12–15 he wrote:

> For there is no difference between Jew and Gentile – the same Lord is Lord of all and richly blesses all who call on Him, for, 'Everyone who calls on the name of the Lord shall be saved'.
>
> How, then, can they call on the one they have not believed in? And how can they believe in the one of whom they have not heard? And how can they hear without someone preaching to them?
>
> And how can they preach unless they are sent?
>
> As it is written, 'How beautiful are the feet of those who bring good news!'

For Paul, the whole of mankind fell within one or other of two categories – Jews or Gentiles. Nevertheless it is clear that 'the same Lord is Lord of all' and salvation comes to *all* mankind only if individuals call on His name. But they cannot call on the Lord's name if they do not know the gospel. Here lies the responsibility of every Christian – bringing the good news to the world. This is entirely consistent with the clear intention of Jesus when He gave His disciples the great commission, 'Go and make disciples of all nations ...' (Matthew 28:19).

So if our inclination is outward, towards the world, we are set in the direction the Lord intends. But if our inclination is inward, avoiding interaction with the world, we are set in an opposing direction to what the Lord requires. If we disobey the Lord we must face the consequences. If we do not look out, we'd better look out – if you see what I mean!

Reluctant heroes

Christians are notorious for avoiding contact with unbelievers. While that is a sweeping generalization, it is largely true. Given the choice between evangelizing and meeting with other Christians, most believers will opt for the second.

Yet the teaching of the New Testament is clear. We need look no further than Jesus' Sermon on the Mount. Matthew 5:13–16 contains a remarkable statement about the position in the world which His disciples should take up:

> You are the salt of the earth. But if the salt loses its saltiness, how can it be made salty again? It is no longer good for anything, except to be thrown out and trampled by men.
>
> You are the light of the world. A city on a hill cannot be hidden. Neither do people light a lamp and

put it under a bowl. Instead they put it on its stand, and it gives light to everyone in the house.

In the same way, let your light shine before men, that they may see your good deeds and praise your Father in heaven.

This is an example of what is called 'parallelism', a device which Jewish rabbis used frequently when they taught and wrote. The idea is that repetition of a theme, expressed in a slightly different way, adds tremendous weight to what is being said.

We find a wonderful example in Luke 15, where Jesus is wanting to demonstrate His attitude to 'sinners' – 'the lost'. Jesus uses three parables, one after the other, to emphasize His point – the parables of the lost sheep, the lost coin and the lost son. Although each parable is placed in a quite different setting, all three have the same basic point: the joy of the Lord over finding a person who had once been 'lost'. In this example of parallelism, Jesus is driving His point home with tremendous force.

So too in Matthew 5, our Lord's use of parallelism is highly significant. The basic point here is obvious: disciples of Jesus need to penetrate the world in the same kind of way salt affects unsavoury things and light overcomes darkness. The mere fact that Jesus uses parallelism to make His point forcefully indicates that the disciples were reluctant to accept it. Little has changed with the centuries!

First, Jesus said, 'You are the salt of the earth.' He was making use of a scene from everyday life to make a crucial point, drawing His illustration from the kitchen. His simple point is that when a woman cooks with salt, it alters the taste of something. Salt is put into *unsavoury* things to make them *savoury*. No cook can achieve this by waving the salt jar at the food from the far side of the kitchen or from the house next door! Unless the salt is put right into the unsavoury food it will have no effect whatever. The unsavoury cannot be affected from a distance.

Second, Jesus said, 'You are the light of the world.' Here our Lord, in making His basic point, uses another illustration from everyday life. He takes His hearers into the living room on a dark evening. What will transform the darkness? Nothing except the introduction of light. Light must be introduced into the dark place otherwise the darkness will remain. If the light is kept at a distance, the darkness will remain dark.

A common objection raised by some well-intentioned Christians is that if you encourage a believer to get involved with people in the world, the world's attitudes will erode the believer's faith. On the face of it this objection might appear sound. It *is* true that the pull of the world has drawn many Christians after it and nullified their faith. But the problem here is not the call of the Lord into the world, but the tendency we have to allow the world into *us*.

To keep to the metaphors used in Matthew 5, salt and light have to remain true to their own natures if they are to function. Unsavoury salt is useless, as is a lamp with no flame! Worldliness removes our saltiness and snuffs out our flame. But if we remain true to the new nature – *God's* nature – which is ours since we received Jesus Christ as Saviour and Lord, we need not fear that we shall stumble.

It is perfectly obvious that salt will not become unsavoury simply because a cook puts it into unsavoury vegetables! The reverse will always be true: the vegetables will become savoury because of the presence of the salt. Similarly it is obvious that the strength of a light placed in a darkened room cannot be reduced by the degree of darkness around it. The reverse will always be true. If a light is switched on after dark in a room with open curtains, the darkness does not intrude through the window and threaten the light: rather, the light streams out through the window shattering the darkness with a great pool of light across the lawn. This should encourage Christians to respond to the call of Jesus and get involved in the world.

... but why the reluctance?

Why would Jesus need to issue a two-line whip to convince His disciples of the need to penetrate the world with the gospel? Surely men and women who are true believers would need no such urging to get out into the world with the good news of the Kingdom of God. Why indeed did Paul need to write in similar vein to the Christians in Corinth?

> I have written to you in my letter not to associate with sexually immoral people – not at all meaning the people of this world who are immoral, or the greedy and swindlers, or idolaters. In that case you would have to leave this world.
>
> But now I am writing to you that you must not associate with anyone who calls himself a brother but is sexually immoral or greedy, an idolater or a

slanderer, a drunkard or a swindler. With such a man do not even eat. (1 Corinthians 5:9–11)

Paul was writing to get the Corinthian believers to associate with people of the world but *not* with *Christians* who were living by worldly standards! This is a vital distinction. The city of Corinth desperately needed the effect of true Christian witness to change it from within. But how could this happen if the Christians hived off and spent all their time with each other? Paul had written to them previously, encouraging the believers to keep clear of people living immoral lives, and the Corinthian Christians immediately jumped to the conclusion that they should keep away from non-believers. That was not Paul's intention! His concern was that they should steer clear of so-called *Christians* who in spite of their boast to be believers were in fact 'Corinthianizing' behind a cloak of piety.

Thank you, Alexander!

Great empires rise, then wax and eventually wane. Their legacies have positive effects upon the world and negative ones. Take the Greek Empire for example. Great art from the time of the ancient Greeks confounds us by its beauty. The Delphi Charioteer, Winged Victory and the Venus de Milo are among the finest sculptures in the world, created by such geniuses as Phidias, Polyclitus and Myron. The architects who conceived the perfection of the great pagan temple of Athena (the Parthenon in Athens) and the Shrine of Apollo at Delphi still challenge modern, lesser mortals who dare to describe their efforts with the same term – the word 'architect' comes from the Greek *archi* (chief) and *tekton* (builder).

Great Greek literature survives – the histories of Herodotus and Thucydides, the poems of Aeschylus, Homer and Sophocles. In the field of philosophy, men like Aristotle, Plato and Socrates still hold court in modern chambers of debate through their ideas, and who among us does not wince at memories of the theorem of Pythagoras!

Yet in among the cultural gems the Greeks bequeathed to the world are items less worthy of applause. In our present debate, one stands out with such clarity that it deserves close examination. It explains a good deal about the reluctance of Christians to be involved out in the world. Once we understand the root of the problem, it will (hopefully) help us to deal with it.

Greek culture was highly developed and deeply rooted by the time Alexander succeeded his father, Philip of Macedon, as emperor, in 336 BC. He was 20 years old. The accumulation of great thought, art and social development through seven centuries had combined to produce the greatness that we associate with Classical Greece. Alexander's vision was to emancipate all the peoples of the world through Greek culture and wisdom and bring in a 'new world order' based on a 'one world' concept.

Alexander the Great, emperor of Greece, was so named for his military exploits. In 334 BC he began a campaign which saw him march into Asia and liberate Greek cities which the Persians had occupied. By this time the Persian Empire was tottering badly and Alexander's brilliance quickly made him victor in the field. When he died in 323 BC, at the age of 33 (a mere eleven years after the start of his campaigns), Alexander left behind an empire that stretched right across the known world, from Europe to India. Romantics delight in saying that Alexander died of a broken heart because he had no more worlds to conquer! The less colourful truth is that he died of a fever which he contracted in Babylon while planning to invade Arabia.

Alexander was highly intellectual. His boyhood mentor was Aristotle, and the famous philosopher imbued him with a love for Greek art and poetry, and instilled in him a lasting interest in philosophy and science. During his military campaigns, Alexander had philosophers accompany him to advise him on political matters.

Alexander's vision was to spread Greek culture throughout the world, much as we exported the British way of life in our colonial days. 'Hellenism' (after Hellas, the Greek name for Greece) became the philosophy of all civilized people and a new world emerged, expansive and cultured. But the liberal spirit of the new age bore down with the force of tyranny upon those like Orthodox Jews whose beliefs were not in harmony with Greek ideas. The traditional faith of Israel was under heavy siege. Following the death of Alexander, the process of Hellenization was pursued by his successors. Israel was ringed by Greek states on the north, east and south and there was a string of nine Greek cities along the west coast.

The impact of Hellenism on Jews and Christians

The years following Alexander's death in 323 BC saw the continuing march of Greek ideas into Jewish life and religion. The empire was shared out between four Greek generals, and Israel was sandwiched between two of them – Seleucus who was based in Syria and Ptolemy who was based in Egypt. To all appearance, Jerusalem became a Greek city, complete with gymnasium, pagan temples and theatres. Plans were afoot to change the city's name to Antioch, in honour of the Syrian Greek king, Antiochus, and only those Jews who were in full sympathy with Hellenism would be considered fit to be citizens. This was a time when young Jewish men in Jerusalem adopted Greek fashion in clothes and when priests could be seen taking part naked in athletics meetings in the Holy City! Orthodox Judaism was scandalized.

Hellenism was very dangerous to Judaism because of its syncretism. It sought to blend religions together. So it was that many Jews adopted pagan practices and yet maintained they were Orthodox!

Things became unendurable in 167 BC when the Syrian Greeks began burning copies of the Jewish Torah and rededicated the Jerusalem Temple in honour of Zeus. The Maccabean Revolt resulted. The Greeks were driven out by the Jews who for close on a hundred years enjoyed independence. Internal wrangling among later Maccabean rulers led to the intervention of Pompey in 63 BC and the Roman occupation of Israel began. Through all the upheavals of the last three centuries before the Romans came, many Hellenists within Jewish society aggressively encouraged Greek thinking and life-style. One expression of this, which was to have far reaching effects on the faith of Jews and Christians, was Gnosticism.

Gnosticism as a philosophical concept developed during the second century AD, but in its primitive form it was highly active in the New Testament period. Paul was continually fighting Gnostic tendencies among the churches and Judaism was riddled with it. Put simply, the Gnostics believed that all things spiritual were innately *good*, while all things physical and material were innately *evil*. This notion found expression in two major forms, quite different from each other, but with a common root.

First, there were those who argued that if only spiritual things are innately good, man must suppress and turn away from all things associated with the material world and the physical body and apply himself as much as possible to the pursuit and promotion of the spiritual. The Greek Stoics subscribed to this. The original Stoics were disciples of the philosopher Zeno who taught in the Painted Porch (*Stoa Poikile*) in Athens during the first half of the third century BC.

To anyone familiar with the Letters of Paul, this form of Gnosticism is instantly recognizable. Paul was continually fighting the belief that true Christianity required a withdrawal from the world and retreat into a kind of Christian ghetto where only spiritual people and spiritual things were encountered. In passages in his letters like 1 Corinthians 5:9–10 and Colossians 2:20–23, Paul is battling to counter Gnostic ideas and to persuade Christians to get back into the world. It is true that Christians must not live as if they *belong* to this world, but it is equally true that they must bear their testimony *within* the world and not hidden away from it.

Second, there were those who espoused Gnostic ideas who took their basic premise and from it formed conclusions diametrically opposed to the Stoical school. The Greek Epicureans (who followed the teaching of Epicurus)

– also known as Hedonists (from the Greek *hedone*, meaning 'pleasure') – subscribed to the idea that if only spiritual things are innately good it must follow that these are the only things which have divine recognition. This being so, the gods must be indifferent to physical matters and worldly things and so man can indulge them as much as he wishes, for such indulgence can have no eternal significance. To the Hedonists, the pursuit of pleasure was the highest good!

Again, we recognize that Paul was continually addressing this tendency to worldliness among Christians. In passages like 1 Corinthians 5:1–13 and 6:9–11, Paul is battling on this second front. His appeal now is for *practical holiness* in the midst of an alien culture. The Christians are simply not permitted to live anyhow and get away with it, much as they might wish to!

Both of these tendencies, with roots in primitive Gnosticism, have been poison to the Church, not least in our own day. The tendency towards presumption upon the grace of God in the matter of personal holiness is all too prevalent. There is precious little true holiness in the lives of most of us and yet we remain unconcerned as if it does not matter. The truth is, it matters desperately. However, if anything, the stoical emphasis has even greater destructive impact on the Church today and goes a long way to explaining our lamentable lack of influence in society.

We draw a false distinction between what we deem to be *spiritual* and what we deem to be *secular*. For instance, we draw a distinction between the jobs people do. Some we consider to be more appropriate for Christians than others. We encourage a young Christian to be a church minister, missionary, evangelist or Bible teacher because we consider these jobs the most spiritual. We then move down a level to professions like medicine, because although not quite like being ministers in the Church, doctors and nurses care for people, and this is very worthy of Christian involvement. Teaching, the police service and social work score fairly highly as well, but none of these quite match up to 'the ministry'. So we think.

The great league table in the sky?

We have a curious tendency to create a kind of 'table of excellence' as regards employment. We believe this is the way God views it. We think that God approves of certain kinds of job and disapproves of others. In this divine disapproval I am not thinking of clearly sub-Christian professions like prostitution, drug-peddling or gun-running (!) but of perfectly respectable jobs which do not fall within our definition of 'Christian ministry'.

It is very easy for us to feel threatened when parents with children who are in so-called 'full-time service' talk about the work they are doing. 'Mary is on the mission-field in Zambia', 'John is serving the Lord as minister of a Baptist church in Macclesfield', 'Sam is working with YWAM ["Youth with a Mission"]', 'Theresa is ...'. You know the sort of thing.

My own three children are in full-time service for the Lord. One is manager of a fitness centre, one is a BBC television presenter and the youngest, who is completing her art training, is also hoping to join the BBC very soon. 'Ah, yes, but surely you mean a *Christian* fitness centre?

Surely you mean *religious* broadcasting? Surely you cannot seriously suggest that as a preacher you have encouraged your children to be out there in the corrupt secular worlds of gyms and television!'

But that is precisely why Lindy and I are so proud of our three. They are out where the action is and they are there serving the Lord in full-time service. I am as proud of Simon, Katy and Naomi as if they were all three full-time evangelists working with Billy Graham. In God's eyes there is no difference! If there *is* a difference, God must be a Gnostic – and He isn't!

The Hebrew way of thinking about life is based firmly upon the Old Testament Scriptures. To the Jewish people, life is *life*. One of their favourite toasts is 'To life!' ('L' Chaim'). A very important theological point is reflected in this attitude – the complete opposite of Gnosticism. In the Bible, the distinction between secular and sacred is virtually non-existent. God is seen to be involved in everything we do. This explains the many Jewish prayers which fit every conceivable occasion. I understand there is even a Jewish prayer which one can say when seated on the lavatory! In it the Lord is praised and thanked for a successful bowel movement. This shocks and offends many Christians who believe God is not interested in such things. To talk about them and specially to *pray* about them is frankly disgusting. But if the Lord created my body to function this way, it does not disgust *Him*! Indeed, as a friend of mine says, if we ever come to the day when our bowels cease to operate, we may well wish we had thanked the Lord more often!

It may put a new slant upon Psalm 139:2, 'You know when I sit and when I rise; you perceive my thoughts from afar.' Some may object that this is a misuse of Scripture. Why so? It offends only if we are trapped by Gnostic thinking.

For some years I worked as principal of a Bible college in the City of London. I was privileged to get to know men and women who were serving the Lord at all levels in banks, offices, the Stock Exchange, Lloyds and Lincoln's Inn. Men and women of varying ability, but all serving the Lord the best way they could, often within very hostile surroundings.

In talking with them a pattern emerged. Although highly effective in their place of work, and often highly placed, the status of these Christian men and women was radically different in the workplace from what it was in their local church. I recall a judge who had served the Lord in the judiciary for many years. His responsibilities were awesome, and he had always striven to maintain his integrity and apply his faith to his decisions. Well and good. But in his local church he counted for very little. He was valued as a good source of revenue, and it was considered something of a 'Brownie point' to have a High Court judge in the congregation, but his Christian ministry was seen as being his limited activity in the church and *not* his magnificent work in the judiciary. He qualifies to be included among what I describe as the 'ecclesiastically disadvantaged'!

The fact is that in many churches a teenager who has been a Christian for six months and takes part in some 'evangelistic outreach' for a fortnight is considered to have a far more valuable 'Christian ministry' than a senior executive who has served the Lord in his difficult profession for thirty years! What a scandal. It offends the whole tenor of the Bible. It is *Greek* thinking, and is diametrically opposed to God's Word.

Paul fought against this way of thinking because it represented a stronghold in the minds of Christians in his day. For Paul it was a matter of spiritual warfare in which the mind is the battlefield. It is for us also. Every thought we have must serve God's Word. If any of our cherished ideas are at variance with the Bible, we have to change them, and change them *immediately*.

Paul got straight to the point when he wrote in 2 Corinthians 10:3–5, 'For though we live in the world we do not wage war as the world does. The weapons we fight with are not the weapons of the world. On the contrary, they have divine power to demolish strongholds.'

But what are these 'strongholds'? He goes on, 'We demolish *arguments and every pretension that sets itself up against the knowledge of God, and we take captive every thought to make it obedient to Christ.'*

So the 'strongholds' are in our minds. They are arguments and ideas which are contrary to the way God sees things. When we are confronted with such unbiblical notions we are to 'demolish' them by replacing them with biblical thinking: making our thoughts and ideas obedient to Jesus Christ.

A Gnostic sense of values?

Greek thinking infects the Christian's attitude and creates double standards. Church buildings and property can sometimes be in a filthy and run-down condition, completely different from standards we maintain in our own homes and places of employment. But, somehow, we tolerate it and find it perfectly acceptable. Neglect can sometimes appear to be everywhere. Dust forming a film of grime over the church furniture, dirty toilets with plaster hanging off the wall, carpets with threadbare patches all over them, rickety or rusty chairs with uncomfortable seats, hymnbooks with the covers falling off ... and so on.

Then we must face the tendency we have to accept terrible standards of worship participation: reading from the Scriptures with scarcely a moment's preparation; allowing people to preach who have no gifting whatsoever, but who simply show willing; encouraging anyone who is prepared to 'have a go' to preach to the congregation or teach Sunday school; allowing cacophonous noise to masquerade as 'worship leading'! The impression given (and perhaps it is not simply an impression) is that we expect God to accept a standard of service which is vastly lower than that which we offer our employer!

People often joke that if you wish to have a decent meal, never go to a Christian guest house or coffee shop, because standards are much lower than in their non-Christian counterparts. Not always true, but often only too true. Why so?

We pay our ministers a pittance when compared with managers in industry, and expect them to be jolly grateful for it! The old American adage, 'Lord, you keep our Pastor humble and we will keep him poor!', is not far off the mark in many a church and chapel. The reason for this general disparity – and it affects so many areas of Christian life – is Gnostic thinking. Because we perceive Church activities as *spiritual* rather than material or physical, we invest them with an 'other-worldliness' and consider that they must be treated by a different set of values, usually a *lower* set of values.

Once we begin to recognize the problem, we are in a position to do something about it. But it is so deep rooted in many of us that only a deep repentance resulting in a firm and radical change of direction in our thinking will redeem the situation. Gnostic thinking and behaviour are an offence to God.

Outreach means reach out

In order to reach out to someone, you have to take a deliberate decision. Breaking out of the Christian ghetto requires a massive effort of will because we have for so long been caged by Gnostic thinking.

Even our evangelism is inverted. We attempt to make our church 'user friendly' and to create an attractive place to which non-believers will wish to come. We arrange 'guest services' and try to make them jargon-free, with no 'cringe factor'. But this is an inversion of our Lord's command that we should go to where the people actually *are*!

How many of us belong to non-Christian organizations from choice, how many make a point of making friends with non-believers, how often do we invite our non-believing neighbours to our homes? The fact is that so much of our time is taken up with what our Gnostic thinking tells us is 'the Lord's work' that we never get around to doing what the *Bible* says is 'the Lord's work'!

Enough said. The world is waiting. Let's go to it!

11
By Way of Apology

At this point I believe I need to apologize and ask for your forgiveness. You may think that strange. Not so strange, when you understand that I am a follower of Jesus Christ and a preacher as well.

Because I have committed my life to Christ I am obliged to speak the truth, the whole truth and nothing but the truth. That includes the truth about him. That's not easy in today's world! Most people seem to think a truly biblical approach to life is ludicrous, anti-social and certainly *passé*! Nevertheless, affront or please, it must be done. I don't really have any choice.

The question is, has God spoken? Has he spoken through the flowers and has he spoken in the 'prophecy'? Is he a communicating God?

God *is* a communicator. But he usually speaks through those he has called to be his spokesmen or spokeswomen. However, it is one thing to have a message from God, it is quite another to deliver it!

As one of God's spokesmen I am bound to declare as clearly as possible what God feels, thinks and says to his world. But it is not my responsibility alone. Indeed, it is the responsibility of the whole Church, especially its leaders –

bishops, vicars and ministers – whatever titles they adopt. Responsibility is one thing, exercising it is another. And from where I sit, most of us Christian leaders appear tongue- and pen-tied. We won't say a thing! So the impression is given that *God* doesn't say a thing!

That is a terrible lie. God is not an absent Father, nor is he a silent Father, he is very much with us and is extremely vocal. But if his messengers refuse to present his messages, people can very understandably doubt that God is even there!

So as far as I am concerned, enough is enough. My guilty silence cannot go on. I cannot be answerable for anyone but myself, but I am answerable for *me*! So, affront or please, it's time for change. Have message, will speak!

A bit of eavesdropping!

Dining out with Lindy is always an interesting experience. Sometimes the food is interesting, sometimes not. But what is always interesting is to observe a glaze come over my dear wife's eyes and to become aware that I do not have her whole attention. The reason for this is the interesting conversation taking place at a nearby table. For Lindy this makes much more fascinating listening than my droning on!

I want to direct these next few paragraphs to my fellow Christians, but those of you who are not committed to Jesus are most welcome to 'listen in' because it concerns you.

The battle for Britain centres around the Church. The primary reason why the country is in its present state of godlessness is that *we Christians have failed the people miserably, and by so doing have failed our Father in heaven*.

We have failed to guard the faith. So-called Christian spokesmen have been permitted to say and write all manner of things which owe more to paganism than to biblical truth. This has gone unchallenged. Because of fear of open opposition we have refused to speak out the truth in the face of error. As a result, millions are misled and face a bleak future without God. Our stated longing for 'unity' with everybody in the 'Church' has been used as an excuse for funk.

Our Gospel is unique. We have good news which no other religion or philosophy possesses. That is not cant, that is fact. But we are so mealy-mouthed about it. Instead of declaring it, we apologize for it. Instead of declaring the fact that Jesus is God, we tell everyone that he is not! Instead of announcing in ringing tones that Jesus died and is alive again, we whimper that we are not sure that he did rise from the dead after all! Instead of shouting from the housetops that Jesus offers mankind the only way to be saved, we cough apologetically and seek, in alliance with other faiths, to present some strange hybrid religion devoid of power and devoid of its heart.

We have failed to declare the utter supremacy and uniqueness of Jesus Christ as the only Lord and Saviour of the world. We have permitted obscenities and blasphemies against him to go unchallenged and have shown so much 'tolerance' of other religious ideas that the clear truth which Jesus declared has been obscured. We have shown a terror of persecution which has locked us into silence when all the time we should have been challenging head-on the false claims of *all* religious views which strip Jesus Christ of his true status as the *only* one who can bring salvation to the world.

We have failed to live as disciples of Jesus Christ. Following Christ requires separation from the values of the world and an embracing of holiness. This we have failed to do. Many who claim to be 'Christian' are scarcely discernible from those who make no such claim. God must be very upset with his Church. Time was when our holy living earned the grudging admiration of our opponents, but not any more. The world has invaded the Church and many of us are happy to have it so. In our mistaken longing to make ourselves relevant to society we have in fact made ourselves *irrelevant,* not only to society but to God as well.

We have failed to penetrate society with the light of Jesus Christ. Gnostic thinking has encouraged us to pursue careers in carefully selected professions which we consider more 'Christian' than others. We have in this way abdicated our responsibilities in key areas of life, principally government, commerce, the media and entertainment. These areas of great influence are left largely to the control of non-Christians and it is scarcely surprising that the values followed are so godless. We have no right to criticize when we stand aloof and choose easier paths for ourselves. We should thank God for the courageous believers who *are* prepared to enter these challenging professions, but all too often such folk are treated by the Church as being tarnished with the world, when all the time it is they who are taking seriously the command of Jesus to be salt in the 'unsavoury' and light in the 'darkness'. How often have we heard well-meaning Christians asking fellow believers working in secular fields, 'When you retire from your company will you be looking to do the Lord's work!' What a put-down! What do they suppose these working people have been doing all these years? Yet it's such a common attitude. God forgive us.

The Jesus of the New Testament *touched* people. In order to do that he had to be near them. Many Christians are so busy maintaining church activities and buildings that they scarcely ever choose to be among the people who need them so desperately. The light is kept under the cover: the salt stays in the cellar.

We Christians have failed to relate our faith to people in need. God has given divine gifts to the Church to enable its members to bless the world in incredibly practical ways, just as Jesus did. He healed people on the streets, he spoke God's word into their lives, those involved in demonic activities were set free. But these miraculous signs of his divine power were not performed only on his disciples, and limited to religious meetings behind closed doors. They were demonstrations of God's amazing love for the *world* and were performed for the most part out in homes, workplaces and hillsides where the people lived, worked and relaxed.

The same thing holds true for the first Christians. Even a casual reading of the Book of Acts will show this to be true. The Gospel was on the streets: the Good News was experienced by the common man as well as declared to him. Jesus Christ changed people – he did not merely impress them. Neither did his disciples. Jesus was alive *in* his followers, and that life communicated itself to all and sundry – particularly the 'sundry'!

We have deprived the people of the living presence of Jesus. We have put him in a box labelled 'church' and given the impression that he can only be found by people daring to run the religious gauntlet and 'going to church'. This is a negation of the gospel. Jesus was and continues to be insistent that his disciples should be out where the people *are*, not in some holy huddle where we rather wish they *might* be.

The Diana focus

For me the clearest example of our sad demise came with the funeral of the Princess of Wales. Countless millions attended the service, either in person in Westminster Abbey or as they watched on television screens in Hyde Park and across the world. They were engaged. They felt a sense of identity. There was silence, there was reverence. People who in other circumstances would not be seen willingly at a Christian service found themselves caught up in a massive one – taking part, reaching out for comfort and revelation of the truth about the Father and the Saviour they do not know.

Ask them now what they remember about the service and they are likely to say two things: Charles Spencer's eulogy for his sister and Elton John's song, *Candle in the Wind*. Why do they not mention the clear proclaiming of the glorious gospel of Jesus Christ which alone can bring salvation and hope? *Because out of fear of reproach the gospel was deliberately left out of the service.*

The two clergy who led the service – Wesley Carr and George Carey, the Dean of Westminster and the Archbishop of Canterbury, no less – steered the nation through a magnificent demonstration of pageantry and piety with no clear reference to the gospel.

True, the Prime Minister read that glorious passage concerning love from chapter 13 of Paul's first letter to the Church in Corinth. True, there were the opening sentences, tremendous verses from the Bible to comfort and encourage the bereft. True, there were scattered references in prayers and biddings to the resurrection of Jesus, but you can scour the reports of that glorious opportunity to comfort and proclaim the saving grace of God in Christ, and I defy you to find one word which clearly enunciated the truth. The entire service was an inoffensive, bland demonstration of what we have become as the Church in Britain – neutered and a disgrace.

It may be objected that at such a service it would have been inappropriate for Christian leaders to take advantage of the situation even if they had wanted to. But that is surely to demonstrate how far we have fallen, when the clear preaching of the gospel is not even *expected* on such an amazing occasion so close to the heart of the nation.

It should also be acknowledged that the service showed a lack of respect for Princes Diana's agnostic position. She demonstrated by her enthusiasm to consult spiritist mediums and by her readiness to empathize with the Moslem and Hindu religions that her commitment to the Christian faith was tenuous at best. We should respect her position. Yet her funeral service included statements which created the impression that she was a committed Christian. Wesley Carr, the Dean of Westminster, actually said in his commendation, 'Diana, our companion in faith and sister in Christ, we entrust you to God ...'

This is highly irresponsible. It is certainly a presumption and in truth borders on insulting when said in such ringing tones of someone who though a remarkable and deeply loving person gave no public indication that she was a committed Christian.

Furthermore, the service made misleading statements about Diana's friend, Dodi Al Fayed. Mr Al Fayed was a committed Moslem. This was his chosen religion. How come, therefore, that George Carey, the Archbishop of Canterbury, should say as part of the prayers: 'Diana was not alone in losing her young life tragically. We remember too her friend, Dodi Fayed and his family ...

'Lord, in certain hope of the resurrection to eternal life, we commend to you all who have lost loved ones in tragic circumstances ...'

In addressing the Lord who gives hope of 'the resurrection to eternal life', and linking Mr Al Fayed's Moslem family with it, the Archbishop was exceedingly patronizing. Islam has no place for the resurrection power of Jesus Christ in its doctrines, and to suggest that it has is insulting to Moslem people. I may have little regard for Islam, but I have every respect for Moslem *people*.

As well as demeaning the beliefs of Princess Diana and her friend, the service created the impression that in spite of having no personal commitment to Jesus Christ, a person can be assured of eternal life in him. Consequently people were left with the impression that even if you live without Christ, you are guaranteed to die with him. This is wishful thinking and has no basis whatsoever in the Bible. None whatsoever!

What was without doubt the greatest evangelistic opportunity in the history of the world, with countless millions across the globe riveted to their television sets, was offered to those two leaders of the Church on that remarkable day. They squandered it out of a misguided desire to be politically correct. Acceptable to society? Perhaps. Acceptable to God? I regret not.

But here we must be very careful. It is thoroughly inappropriate for non-Anglicans to point the finger at the Dean and Archbishop and congratulate ourselves that we are not as other men are! The reason for the pathetic lack of conviction in the Abbey is only a reflection of the pathetic lack of conviction in all of us – whatever our particular denomination. If any significant part of the Church was truly expressing the dynamic power of the Lord out in the public arena where it really matters, it would impact the entire Church. Choices would have to be made. But as things stand, irrespective of the kind of Sunday clothes we wear, we all of us have to shoulder a measure of responsibility for what did not happen in Westminster Abbey on that tragic summer day in September 1997.

I am quite convinced that God is calling the Christians of Britain to return to him and to seek his forgiveness through wholehearted repentance. This word 'repentance' has had a very bad press, and has become little more than a joke word in our vocabulary. But it is the key. The word means 'change of mind after due consideration and remorse'.

May God give us grace to change our whole mind-set and turn back to the true faith of our fathers – believing and living in the Bible, giving wholehearted witness to the only gospel which can save, that of Jesus Christ and Him crucified. It is the only answer. It always has been and it always will be.

We have failed our people, but it is not too late for change. When true faith is absent from the people, it is not that they believe *nothing*. They will believe *anything* as long as it is attractively packaged. It is no use Christians feeling complacent in the situation, and trusting in the mercy of God to 'let us off'. Peter, the apostle, expressed the mind of God when he wrote, 'For the time has come for judgement to begin with the household of God' (1 Peter 4:17).

In similar vein, the final writer of the Old Testament, the prophet Malachi, said,

> For the lips of a priest ought to preserve knowledge, and from his mouth men should seek instruction – because he is the messenger of the Lord Almighty. But you have turned from the way and by your teaching have caused many to stumble; you have violated the covenant with Levi [the priestly covenant],' says the Lord Almighty, 'So I have caused you to be despised and humiliated before all the people, because you have not followed my ways but have shown partiality in matters of the law.'

The penalty we Christians have paid and are paying for failing to proclaim the clear, unequivocal Word of God is that our people despise the Church and we are humiliated at every turn. We can moan and groan all we like, but God's prophet makes it clear that when biblical conditions apply, biblical consequences follow. Our state before the nation is the consequence of our unfaithfulness. It is, in truth, the judgement of God.

We Christians need the forgiveness of God, but we also need to seek the forgiveness of the British people whom we have failed so badly.

'I vow to thee, my country ...'

So begins a great hymn by Cecil Spring-Rice. It was a favourite of Princess Diana and was included in her funeral service. The first verse speaks of serving our country with unreserved love. You can understand why she regarded the hymn so highly: it expressed so much of her. Diana loved Britain and the British people and her love spilled over across the world, especially to the deprived and those without love.

Love for people made Diana reach out to them, to give them what she had to give. To have failed to do that would have been an act of self betrayal, for this was her heart.

As I write these words I am immensely moved and challenged. Princess Diana's example provokes me. It provokes me because as a Christian preacher I have an obligation – to my Lord but also to you. *He* loves the world, and if he loves the world, *I* must love it too. *He* loved the world enough to die for it. I ought at least to love it enough to tell it the truth. He has told me in no uncertain terms that if I consider myself his disciple, I am obliged to speak the truth, the whole truth and nothing but the truth about *him* and about his love for *you*. This I have failed to do. Admittedly, it is a failure I share with many other Christians, but what they do about it is up to them. I have to be true to myself.

At the risk of appearing sloppily sentimental, I ask you, whoever you are, to forgive me. I do not know you, but that is of no consequence. My Lord – Jesus Christ – gave clear instructions in the New Testament that as one of his followers I must proclaim the gospel to every person I can. That's a pretty tall order. It may not win many friends, but it will certainly influence a good many – probably to dislike me!

The fact is, I have not done what I am required to do. Why not? It may be fear of opposition. It probably is. It may be fear of rejection and even suffering – it probably is. But one thing is for sure – it shows a lack of love for you. And that is the point. I have not loved you enough to risk your rejection. I have cared more about my own skin than about your eternal salvation. That is a desperately serious matter and I ask you to forgive me.

I know a man who was a Royal Air Force chaplain for a number of years. When new recruits arrived at his base, they were required to indicate their religion on the application form. Most put 'C of E' or 'RC' and were immediately placed under the care of the Anglican or Catholic chaplains. My friend got all the rest! This group included men who professed to belong to non-Christian faiths, as well as Baptists, Methodists, Congregationalists, Pentecostals ... and atheists!

My friend enjoyed interviewing the atheists. When talking with them he was always careful to say that he respected them for their *faith*, because he maintains it took far more faith to believe what they did about the origins of the world than it did to believe that a great creative mind lay behind it all!

He also assured the atheists that his respect for their 'belief' that there is no God was so genuine that if they were killed in action or by accident or died of some sickness while in his care he would guarantee them an atheist's funeral. There would be a eulogy from a relative or friend, perhaps a favourite poem or piece of music might be performed, but there would definitely be no hymns, no prayers, no reading from the Bible – in fact, no mention of God at all.

My friend told me that their reaction to this was often very dramatic. So he concluded that while there are many people who are prepared to live without God, they are not so happy to *die* without him. Unfortunately, to leave the matter of one's eternal salvation until the moment when death approaches, is to leave it too late.

I recall something else my RAF friend told me. He would ask atheists to tell him about this God they didn't believe in! Their replies usually showed that they had little or no understanding of the truth about him as we find it in the Bible. Theirs was a caricature of God, cobbled together from many sources over the years. My friend would listen attentively and then say, 'Well that must make *me* an atheist too, because I don't believe in that God either! Would you like to know about the God I *do* believe in?'

They usually said, 'Yes please!' Many of them lost their atheism there and then and found salvation in Jesus Christ.

'Who *are* you, Father?'

My maternal grandfather served in the trenches during the First World War and had never seen one of his sons that my grandmother had borne him while he was away from home. By the time he returned in 1918, the child was nearly four years old. As my grandfather walked through the village and approached the old home, a round-faced little boy ran up to him and, greeting him as a total stranger, asked, 'Got a cigarette card, mister?'

That little boy was my uncle. Just as he did not know his own father, but saw him as a total stranger, so many of us fail to relate to our heavenly Father. This little family anecdote touches deep chords. Scale it up to the eternal dimension and you begin to glimpse the utter pathos of the situation when so many people do not know their heavenly Father.

In the Old Testament book of Psalms, the Lord God shows glimpses of himself in many moving passages, none more so than in the first eighteen verses of Psalm 139. The writer of the Psalm, King David of Israel, was inspired to write these amazing lines:

O Lord, you have searched me and you know me.
You know when I sit and when I rise;
You perceive my thoughts from afar.
You discern my going out and my lying down;
You are familiar with all my ways.
Before a word is on my tongue you know it completely,
    O Lord.

David says that he can never find himself in any situation where his heavenly Father would leave him, and then in verse 13 he goes on,

For you created me in my inmost being,
You knit me together in my mother's womb.
I praise you because I am fearfully and wonderfully
    made:
Your works are wonderful, I know that full well.
My frame was not hidden from you when I was made in
    the secret place.

When I was woven together in the depths of the earth,
 your eyes saw my unformed body.
All the days ordained for me were written in your book
 before one of them came to be

This is so remarkable! The Lord God shows David that he put him together quite deliberately. David could never say, 'I was never really *wanted*!' because God wanted him! In his care the Lord God planned and prepared for each one of us. There is no one who is a 'nobody' in God's eyes. We are all special to him and it breaks his heart when we try to live as if he were not there.

This is the God who reveals the truth about himself in the Bible. He cares about *you*. He loved you so much that although your rebellion against him and indifference towards him deserve only his judgement, he made a way for you to be totally changed. A way for you to be completely forgiven: a way in which you can move out from the devil's prison into the true freedom of God's sons.

Our heavenly Father has made a way for you to have eternal life here and now, as well as after your physical death. He has made a way for you to be filled with his power to enable you to come through your circumstances – through personal faith in Jesus Christ as Lord.

12
Go Back to Go Forward

It should be obvious to thinking people that there is an incredible battle going on in our society – a battle for people's minds. The protagonists are, in fact, Almighty God and Satan. This sounds an incredible statement reflecting a world-view long dead, but it happens to be the truth, if we are to believe what we read in the Bible.

It is a *spiritual* battle, but its effects can be seen in the world of time and space. The evidence is all around, some of it very obvious – wars, racial hatred, child abuse, marriage breakdown, false religion and cults, violence, anarchy, drug abuse, pornography, the occult, disease, sexual perversion, satanic oppression and even demonization.

But perhaps the clearest evidence for this battle is more personal and certainly more subtle. It is this that fuels the more obvious fires. Things like pride, ambition, lust, greed are all part of the human condition. The truth is we are never free of them. There is a tendency in people to want to rebel against God and his values and the consequences are all around.

Destructive forces are at work which have not only eroded decent values but have all but destroyed many of them. This is not aimed merely at introducing an alternative, permissive life-style. It is a head-on attempt to remove God from his world and replace him with Satan. It is as stark as that.

Ignoring the existence of the enemy is the surest way to be defeated

This conflict of the ages has never been more obvious than today. But most folk seem woefully unaware of its seriousness. They even refuse to recognize it and consider such suggestions to be the rantings of the criminally insane.

Such is the condition of the Christian Church in this country that many senior ministers of every denomination appear to identify with this attitude. They seek in every possible way to denude the Word of God of its power and replace it with their own woefully inadequate opinions.

Jesus had personal experience of the devil and had more to say about hell than he did about heaven, but it is now fashionable among churchmen to laugh to scorn anyone who dares to suggest that there is a devil or that hell is an actual place.

The impression is given that God (if He exists at all) is a kind of absentee landlord who is frankly indifferent to what goes on in His world and so permits people to live as they choose. They can take the high moral ground or grovel about in the low moral ground – it actually makes no difference. As long as we don't interfere with each other's preferences we can live pretty much as we like.

Hang on a minute ...

Media pundits and social commentators delight in telling us that Christian values in general and the Bible in particular have now all but passed out of British life. But having said that, there is a detectable sense of unease and even outrage among a growing number of normal people, who frankly do not agree. More and more people are saying, enough is enough. We have been sitting idly by for far too long. Indifference does not immunize us from destructive forces at work in our midst. It guarantees that we shall fall victims to them. Evil prospers when good people do nothing. To some extent our journey to the 'brave new world' felt like a great adventure, but now it becomes increasingly clear that it is a headlong rush into anarchy and chaos.

Was this sense of outrage at what we have become one of the reasons for the tide of grief which swept over us at the time of Diana's death? It is an interesting and heart-searching question.

People were reaching out for something firm, something to comfort them in their grief for Diana and for themselves. Was this what it all comes to in the end? A pile of rotting flowers and a tolling, muffled bell?

The golden thread

Woven into the life fabric of Diana, Princess of Wales, was a brightly shining thread, constantly visible, winding in and out of all the richly coloured shades and gorgeous textures. It was a longing to be loved and to love in return.

Tragedy early in life deprived her of the normal love of parents. Tragedy in marriage deprived her of the love of her husband who would one day be king. The observation of her despair resulting from this twin loss has filled acres of printed paper and miles of recording tape. It has fascinated us all.

Public fascination has been guaranteed because the Princess's despair mirrors that of so many people. But it goes far beyond the human dimension. It takes us into levels of ultimate reality – our relationship with God.

The waiting Father

We have a longing for the love of our Father in heaven, whether we care to admit it or not. Irrespective of our upbringing – whether Christian or otherwise – the lack of a personal, intimate relationship with God leaves us without hope, deprived of His love and abandoned. This is not some sentimental twaddle, this is the stuff of biblical revelation. It is Ultimate Truth – God's Truth.

And the news is good. Very good. Almighty God stands ready and waiting to adopt us as His children, to lavish His love upon us, if we will have it.

I am not by nature a child of God. The Fall has seen to that. Iniquity has formed a complete barrier between me and God. I cannot know Him, I cannot see Him, I cannot find Him. But in His unfathomable love for me, God has made a way for the devastating effects of the Fall to be undone. It all centres on His Son, our Lord Jesus Christ.

Jesus came. He died and was buried, in my place. God laid all *my* iniquity on *Him*. Jesus died in place of me. So my iniquity has been removed in the death of Jesus Christ. The result of this is that salvation is possible for me *if* I grasp hold of it by faith. This I must do for myself. No one can do it for me.

Our Father stands waiting for our return. His grace and love, lavished on us in eternal measure, fills us with hope, overwhelms us in peace and replaces our sense of abandonment with the certainty that we are utterly secure in the arms of God.

The divine husband

Christians – both male and female – have a longing for a husband who is a king! This strange comment springs directly from the New Testament, where the relationship between Jesus Christ and the Church is regularly described as that of a husband and his bride.

The love between a husband and his wife is the highest emotion known to man. This is one reason why the metaphor is used by God to describe His Son and His Church, but even then it cannot express it fully. The relationship which exists and will exist between the Church and Christ is so sublime that even the most perfect human marriage doesn't come close!

Since His ascension to heaven, Jesus Christ has been preparing the extension to His Father's house to accommodate His 'bride', the Church. The Church, in her turn, to the extent that its members have sought to live holy lives, has through the centuries been preparing herself for His return for her, motivated with a burning longing, 'Come, Lord Jesus!'.

How great is the tragedy when a 'bride-to-be' has little or no excitement that her bridegroom is soon coming for her. What kind of love is this? What kind of love is it that can be so easily diverted to secondary issues? Many Christians are scarcely aware that Jesus Christ is soon coming for His Church. Their focus is elsewhere. They are captivated with thoughts of impending revival, or with the notion that everything will continue just as it is for aeons to come! These deceptions leave many Christians quite unprepared for the return of Christ.

But even Christians who are anticipating the return of the Lord rather hope that He does not come back too soon because they have 'plans to make and places to go'! Young people want to get married and have children before He comes! Older people hope to have at least some years of retirement in which to enjoy their old age pension before He comes!

Such reactions betray a hope which is wrongly focussed. Those who have a deep love for Jesus Christ can only long for Him to come – the sooner the better! – like a besotted young bride longing for her husband to come for her!

Don't mention the King

The Millennium is upon us. We are being persuaded that it is a most significant moment in the story of mankind. Billions of pounds will be spent on elaborate buildings and all kinds of commemorative marketing devices will be brought to bear on this great moment, to milk it for all it's worth.

But why the clamour? What are we supposed to be celebrating? Most people do not appear to know! It is an insane, massive and incredible birthday party held in honour of a person we are not even supposed to mention in the celebrations because it is not considered 'politically correct'! But it is precisely this attitude which has created the heart-rending, gut-wrenching anguish in the hearts of millions.

We Christians must bring King Jesus back to the people. Let us declare it loud, and let us declare it long – we are celebrating the two thousandth anniversary of the human birth of the King of Kings, Jesus Christ our Lord, God the Son, our only Saviour, who died and is alive for evermore! Furthermore, we declare that he is soon returning to planet Earth to set up his kingdom and receive the homage of the entire universe.

The Flowers in the Cities came, and they have gone. Their fragrance and beauty haunted us and the messages they bore expressed emotions deeper than words. The flowers faded, their fragrance turned sour. Even the memory of Diana will recede with the years.

But Jesus Christ is the same yesterday, today and for ever. He brings a joy that will never diminish, a love that never fails, a secure hope that nothing can threaten ... *if* we will receive Him and acknowledge Him as Lord and King.

The grass withers and the flowers fall,
but the word of our God stands for ever. (Isaiah 40:8)